EXILE

EXILE

Pramoedya Ananta Toer
in conversation with
Andre Vltchek and Rossie Indira

Foreword by Chris GoGwilt

Edited by Nagesh Rao

Haymarket Books
Chicago, Illinois

Exile: Conversations with Pramoedya Ananta Toer
First published in 2006 as *Saya Terbakar Amarah: Pramoedya Ananta Toer dalam Perbincangan dengan Andre Vltchek & Rossie Indira* in Indonesia by Kepustakaan Populer Gramedia.

Published in 2006 by Haymarket Books
PO Box 180165
Chicago, IL 60618
773-583-7884
www.haymarketbooks.org

Cover design by Ragina Johnson
Printed in Canada

Library of Congress Cataloging in Publication Data

Toer, Pramoedya Ananta, 1925–
Exile : conversations with Pramoedya Ananta Toer / Andre Vltchek and Rossie Indira ; edited by Nagesh Rao.
    p. cm.
ISBN-13: 978-1-931859-28-8
ISBN-10: 1-931859-28-0
1. Indonesia—Politics and government—1950–1966. 2. Indonesia—Politics and government—1966–1998. 3. Indonesia—Politics and government—1998– 4. Toer, Pramoedya Ananta, 1925– I. Title: Conversations with Pramoedya Ananta Toer. II. Vltchek, Andre. III. Indira, Rossie. IV. Rao, Nagesh. V. Title.
    DS644.4.T675 2006
    959.803--dc22

                                    2006008706

10 9 8 7 6 5 4 3 2 1

Contents

Foreword

Chris GoGwilt

In this extended conversation with Pramoedya Ananta Toer, Andre Vltchek and Rossie Indira bring us the voice of Indonesia's most celebrated writer, author of the internationally acclaimed "Buru Quartet" of novels and a towering figure in world literature. Pram (as he is generally called) speaks here with characteristic directness, confronting the circumstances of historical, political, and inhuman oppression with the voice of individual experience, personal conviction, and human spirit. What Pram says is moving, and at times painfully so. Following everything he has experienced, from his beginnings as a writer under Dutch imprisonment in the late 1940s through the period of his exile on Buru Island under the "New Order"* regime, it is striking to learn that Indonesia's greatest living writer still describes his present condition as one of "internal exile."

After long years of imprisonment and exile on Buru following the events of 1965, Pram remained under house ar-

* See Glossary

rest, his voice silenced and his books censored, until after the collapse of Suharto's New Order regime in 1998. Since then, books that had been published and banned under the New Order regime have become available to an Indonesian readership within Indonesia. Outside Indonesia, his works have become increasingly available in translation. In 1999, permitted to leave Indonesia for the first time in over thirty years, he toured the United States and Europe, hailed as a dissident voice no longer silenced. Both within Indonesia and in the international press, he is often cited as Indonesia's greatest writer. Indeed, only recently a news report portrayed Pram as a writer content with his lot and at peace with the world.[1] How, then, can his present condition be one of "internal exile"?

Pram's remarks here offer an extended answer to that question, beginning and ending with the comment that he is still "burning inside" when he thinks of Indonesia. This pent-up fire unfolds over the course of the conversation into a political indictment of contemporary consumer society, endemic corruption, cultural bankruptcy, and historical amnesia. These corrosive features are not, of course, unique to Indonesia; indeed, the distinctive features of what Pram here calls the corruption and decay of Indonesian society put on display, rather, the characteristic fruits of globalization. It is notable, however, that Pramoedya reserves his harshest indictment for Indonesia itself. For Indonesian readers, it may be hard to accept the severity of Pram's critique. For a non-Indonesian readership beyond Indonesia, it may be too easy to dismiss its relevance for the rest of the world. In either case, though, Pram's voice demands to be heard because it speaks urgently, as it always has in all his writings, of the vexed mutual interdependence of Indonesia and the world. "What can I say about the world?" Pram asks toward the end of this book, in anticipation of the question of "internal exile": "We hardly know anything about the world here, and the world knows nothing about Indonesia." That formulation itself captures the double bind of Pram's sense of "internal exile."

The directness and immediacy with which Pram's literary voice addresses its reader—whether in Indonesian or in translation—typically involves a performative balance of personal experience against the political and historical coordinates of that experience. His early story, "Blora," for example, creates its autobiographical first-person narrative voice by hailing the author's name from within the Dutch prison (*Bukit Duri*) from which Pram's first published work emerged ("The jailer returned from the camp office and yelled, 'Pram!' I yelled back in response. And he went on, 'You're being released.'"[2]) Pram's conversational voice in these conversations should not, of course, simply be conflated with the narrative voice of his literary work. Nonetheless, there is a significant relationship between the two. As Goenawan Mohamad puts it in his foreword to the English translations of *Tales from Djakarta: Caricatures of Circumstances and Their Human Beings*, Pramoedya's prose "engages his reader in a constant conversation, establishing a context defined by a shared sense of experiencing 'Indonesia.'"[3] That context (*Tales from Djakarta* was originally published in

1957) has since undergone a number of drastic changes, and it is Pram's adjustment to those changes that makes the whole body of his work so significant and indispensable a contribution to world literature: from the period of revolutionary anticolonial nationalism ("Blora" comes from this moment), through the late 1950s and the period of disillusionment with postcolonial nation building (the period of *Tales from Djakarta*) and, with the catastrophe of 1965, the reversal of revolutionary nationalism and the setting up of the New Order Indonesia (the period of Pram's dissident Buru writings, most notably the "Buru Quartet").

Throughout, Pram has sought to engage the reader in a constant conversation about the experience of Indonesia, even in the absence of a readership (as captured in the prison notes partially translated into English under the evocative title *The Mute's Soliloquy*). That history of engagement—and most especially the history of Pram's exile from an Indonesian readership under the New Order regime—makes this set of conversations from 2004 all the more urgent, even as it complicates our response. If Pram, since 1965, has had to address a substantially absent readership, our own present response to Pram's voice, as Indonesian and non-Indonesian readers, needs to come to terms with that absence, as we consider the force of Pram's sense of "internal exile," and as we negotiate that double bind of mutual ignorance linking Indonesia to the world.

It is in this context that we might measure the personal, political, and literary significance of Pram's consistent critique of "Javanism": that "unthinking loyalty and obedience to a superior" that "eventually leads to fascism." This critique extends from the most personal of questions (for example, his relationship to his own family) to questions of language, politics, and history (Javanese, Indonesian, and world history), all of which occupy a central place in his literary works. How, for example, are we to read Pram's judgment here that "There is no hunger for knowledge" in present-day Indonesia? It's a judgment elaborated around a personal criticism of his own family: "my children and grandchildren don't read newspapers anymore. I can't understand it.... They've lost the culture of reading, and prefer watching television. I think that most Indonesian families are the same. They just glue themselves to the television. There is no hunger for knowledge." This isn't only the voice of a grandfather lamenting the fact that his grandchildren are glued to the TV—although it is that, too. In addition, it carries the weight of a personal and historical experience of what is at stake in a "culture of reading." It would be wrong to equate this lament with the kind of cultural conservatism that decries the erosion of a "high" culture through contamination with "low" culture. Pram's conception of literature is the antithesis of belle-lettristic, as is already suggested by the example of the newspaper as a medium for that "culture of reading" whose loss is marked by the televisual medium. Pram's choice of the television as an emblem of consumer culture may be informed by a longer history and greater familiarity with technology than is obvious here. In *The Mute's Soliloquy,* Pram recalls how, at the outbreak of the Second World War, he was struggling to earn a degree from the Radio Vocational School in Surabaya—having to prepare for the practical exams "the diagram of a television, an instrument not widely known at that time."[4] This vocational training, interrupted by the declaration of war, informs his later work as a writer always engaged in the effort to create a means of communication. Pram's antipathy toward TV viewing is not, then, only a grandfather's lament, but might be viewed as part of the wider criticism of the Javanese for not being "productive"—"all they know is how to consume." These contrasts between production and consumption, and between print and televisual media, however, ought not to obscure the sense in which writing—and above all, writing in Bahasa Indonesia—is primarily, for Pram, a means of communication rather than an aesthetic form; a part of that ongoing struggle to engage in a conversation with his reader about the experience of "Indonesia."

When, in the later 1950s and early 1960s, Pram's literary energies turned more toward history, he began republishing articles and stories from the late nineteenth and early twentieth centuries (in the newspaper *Lentera,* in biographies of Kartini and Tirto Adi Suryo, and in an anthology of "pre-Indonesian literature," *Tempo Doeloe,* published later in 1982). These efforts both to reconstruct a past history and to create a new Indonesian culture of reading lie at the core of the Buru tetralogy of novels, for which Pram is perhaps best known internationally. When Pram speaks of a lost culture of reading, then, one might well consider this in relation to the loss on which the Buru tetralogy is premised: the events of 1965, Pram's arrest, and the confiscation and destruction of his manuscripts (as Pram discusses here); and thus, in turn, the loss of that historical record of early Indonesian nationalism that the Buru tetralogy recaptures in fictional form. A precondition for such a culture of reading is, as Pram indicates throughout these conversations, the keeping of historical records. An emblem of this ideal is the plan to complete "an encyclopedia of the Indonesian archipelago," something about which Pram has often spoken in the past.[5] If that appears here as an unrealizable goal ("but I can't finish that work, either"), there is nothing simply idealized about the project. Although it is not clear precisely what shape such an encyclopedia might take, one might consider the example of the three-volume *Kronik Revolusi Indonesia* (1999), which Pram edited together with Koesalah Soebagyo Toer and Ediati Kamil, chronicling events from the years 1945 to 1947.

The personal, political, and historical circumstances of Pram's "internal exile" provide few consolations. Yet Pram's ability to give voice to what is "burning" inside him does serve as provocation: certainly, and above all, as a provocation to take stock of Indonesia's current position in the world. What Pram calls "Javanism" reflects on the present circumstances, but also on Pram's long-standing efforts to reconceive the coordinates of the historical record with respect to Indonesia. The scope of this vision is considerable. It involves the entire twentieth century and the global-historical shock of that century's experience of decolonization, to which Pram's work as a whole stands as the paradigmatic literary testament. Writing back to the roots of Indonesian nationalism, and as a direct consequence of his engagement with the process of decolonization, revolutionary anticolonial nationalism, and the vicious cycle of postcolonial disillusionment with nation building, Pram's work takes us back further: not only to the nineteenth century but also to the sixteenth century, the setting of a long historical novel, *Arus Balik,* first published in 1995 and not yet translated into English. Pram's historical vision reaches back further still—to the thirteenth century, the historical setting for another historical novel, *Arok Dedes,* composed on Buru but not published in Indonesian until 1999 and (again) still not translated into English. Like the Buru tetralogy, these novels extend that effort Goenawan Mohamad described as Pram's engaging a reader in a constant conversation about Indonesia. They extend, too, the long-standing critique of "Javanism" that Benedict Anderson once styled Pram's "crossing swords" with the ossified forms of his Javanese heritage.[6] Such work has yet to find its readers, and so we cannot appreciate the full extent of Pram's success in reconceiving the coordinates of "Javanism," Indonesia, and world history. There is, nonetheless, a direct connection between the "burning" urgency with which Pram speaks out from "internal exile" in these conversations, and the voice that has consistently worked to attempt to produce a culture of reading in Indonesian and about Indonesia in the towering achievement of his literary work.

Thanks to Andre Vltchek and Rossie Indira, Pram's voice comes through loud and clear. Yet it is hardly a voice at peace with the world. What is recorded in *Exile* is a continuation of what Pram has always voiced in his writing—dissidence, defiance, challenge, the uncompromising insistence on freedom and reason, and that individualism called simply "Pramism."

Fordham University
May 2005

1. M. Taufiqurrahman, "Pramoedya now lives peaceful, venerable life," *Jakarta Post*, February 11, 2005.

2. "Blora," translated into English by Harold Merrill, *Indonesia* 53 (April 1992): 51–64; 51. The story was first published in Dutch translation in *Oriëntatie* 26, November 1949, and in the original Indonesian in *Subuh: Tjerita-tjerita pendek revolusi* (DjakartJajasan Pembangunan, 1950).

3. Pramoedya Ananta Toer, *Tales from Djakarta: Caricatures of Circumstances and Their Human Beings* (Ithaca, N.Y.: Southeast Asia Program Publications, 1999), 9.

4. Pramoedya Ananta Toer, *The Mute's Soliloquy: A Memoir* (New York: Penguin, 1999), 149.

5. And something mentioned, too, in the *Jakarta Post* article cited above.

6. "Pramoedya's bahasa Indonesia is a cultural fortress from which to cross swords with his heritage," in Benedict Anderson, *Language and Power: Exploring Political Cultures in Indonesia* (Ithaca, N.Y.: Cornell University Press, 1990), 219.

Introduction

Nagesh Rao

I have so much to say. I want to speak about the young genera-
tions and about the students who fought until Suharto was
forced to resign. I want to speak about other times, the occasions
when people were hunted down, killed, and dumped into the
sea. I have no access to the media and no organization to sup-
port me. I am burning inside. You came here so we can talk, so
now I can open up and bother you with all the frustrations and
curses that have accumulated inside me over long decades.

Thus begins this extraordinary conversation with Indonesia's
literary giant, Pramoedya Ananta Toer. This is the first ever
book-length interview with Pramoedya, a novelist and writer
widely regarded as the artist who gave expression to a revolutionary vision of Indonesian cultural identity. Fusing anticolonial nationalism, humanism, and epic narratives into literary
masterpieces, Pramoedya's works rank among those by the
finest of modern writers, alongside the novels of Salman
Rushdie, Gabriel García Márquez, and Naguib Mahfouz. If

Pramoedya is not quite so well known in literary and academic circles in the West, it is because of the extraordinary conditions of exile, imprisonment, censorship, and repression that he has had to work under. His relative obscurity—outside the circles of Indonesia and Southeast Asia specialists—is also a consequence of the sordid history of cozy relations between the U.S. ruling establishment and the dictatorship of General Suharto.

Exiled for ten years on the Buru Island internment camp and now too weak to write any longer, here is a writer who is still "burning inside," carrying within him an undying passion for truth, justice, and human dignity. Like Rushdie, García Márquez, Mahfouz, and other writers of the post-colonial era, Pramoedya writes with a deep sense of the currency of history, so a brief outline of this history might help the uninitiated reader to get a better grasp of the issues that Pramoedya raises in these conversations with Andre Vltchek and Rossie Indira.

The Scramble for Asia

The Dutch conquest and control of the East Indies was part of a long historical process that saw virtually all of Asia come under the control of the newly emerging capitalist states of Europe. This first phase of European expansion and conquest of Asia dates roughly from 1500 to 1850, 350 years that were characterized by an increasingly frenzied rivalry among the emerging European powers to capture larger and larger portions of the flourishing Asian trade in spices, silk, and tea. For centuries before the development of capitalism

in Europe, India, China, and the Southeast Asian archipelago that we know today as Indonesia had been flourishing
centers of trade, commerce, and culture. With trade routes
cutting across the whole of Asia and Europe, and reaching
even to the west coast of Africa, India and China were, by
the time of the European Middle Ages, far ahead of western
Europe in commercial and technological development. The
historian K. M. Panikkar writes that "[a]fter the early Cru-
sades Europe's interest in Asia increased greatly and both
Venice and Genoa possessed detailed knowledge of Indian
conditions and trade."[1] Centuries later, Hegel noted that
"India as a land of Desire formed an essential element in
general history. From the most ancient times downwards, all
nations have directed their wishes and longings to gaining
access to the treasures of this land of marvels.... The way by
which these treasures have passed to the West has at all times
been a matter of world historical importance."[2]

By the fifteenth century, Muslim traders and merchants
had a virtual monopoly on the flourishing spice trade, due to
the immense power and prestige of the Turkish Ottoman
empire in West Asia, and later the Persian Safavid empire
and the Mughal empire farther east. Panikkar writes: "From
the time of Saladin, who recaptured Jerusalem from the Cru-
saders in 1187, Islam based on Egypt had been organized as
an immensely powerful barrier between Asia and Europe."[3]
European merchants had thus been looking for a sea route to
the Indian Ocean that would allow them to bypass the land
routes that were monopolized by the Arabs. When, in 1498,
the Portuguese sailor Vasco da Gama arrived at the western

coast of India, he fulfilled a two-hundred-year-old dream of European merchants and traders. This particular expedition, financed by the Portuguese king, Dom Manuel, had taken eleven long months to make the voyage around the Cape of Good Hope.

There was little doubt in the minds of the European traders that control of the sea routes would guarantee them immense profits, and they had reason enough to think so. For instance, when Ferdinand Magellan's ship, *Victoria*, circumnavigated the globe in 1521, it stopped off in Sumatra (part of Indonesia today) and loaded up its holds with cloves, which Magellan then sold for a profit of 2,500 percent in Europe.[4] Profit was guaranteed to those who controlled the flow of goods, rather than their actual production. Traders from all over Europe began to set out to follow in da Gama's wake, with the Dutch, the British, and the French arriving at different points throughout the sixteenth and seventeenth centuries. Their eyes were set on three key regions: India, Indonesia (and the Malay Peninsula), and China.

At first, the foreign traders were cautiously welcomed, and in many instances were allowed to set up trading posts in various coastal regions. Where they were not welcomed, they forced their way in, as for instance in 1511, when the Portuguese soldier Afonso Albuquerque arrived in Malacca with a fleet of eighteen ships.[5] Before opening negotiations with the sultan of Malacca, he burnt the ships lying in the harbor and provoked the sultan into an attack. After defeating the sultan, Albuquerque's forces ransacked the city, massacring its inhabitants. Those who survived the massacre were sold into slavery, and the plunder of the city yielded no less than two hundred thousand gold cruzados for the king of Portugal.

The history of these early years of European expansion is full of such stories of murder, death, and destruction, on the one hand, and intrigue and subterfuge, on the other. Where they could, the European traders bribed, cajoled, and deceived their way into obtaining trading rights; where necessary, they looted and plundered. And in all instances, the various European traders were competing not only with local merchants, but with one another as well. The traders and merchants were thus constantly involved in military actions and had to combine commerce with warfare to get their way. The French, the Portuguese, and the British tried to elbow one another out of India. The Portuguese and the Dutch, and later the Dutch and the British, fought numerous short wars for control of the Indonesian islands. To some degree, these wars were a projection overseas of bitter rivalries that were exploding at home. Thus the Dutch war of independence against Spain, which lasted eighty years, from 1568 to 1648, was one of the factors that pushed the Netherlands to expand overseas. As M. C. Ricklefs points out, "The Dutch had acted as middlemen in retailing spices from Portugal in northern Europe, but the war and the union of the Spanish and Portuguese crowns in 1580 disrupted their access to spices brought from Asia by the Portuguese. This naturally only increased their desire to ship spices from Asia themselves."[6] The first Dutch expedition to the East Indies set sail in 1595, and by 1602, various competing Dutch firms merged to form the United East India Company, known by its Dutch initials, VOC.

Dutch rule over the East Indies was characterized by the most repugnant racism. In the coming years, as virtually the entire population of Sumatra, Java, and Borneo was forced into plantation-based slave labor, the democratic ideals of the bourgeois revolutions of France and Holland were not considered applicable to the people of the East Indies. The government in Holland declared: "The doctrines of liberty and equality … cannot be transferred to nor applied to the East Indian possessions of the State so long as the security of these possessions depends on the existing and necessary state of subordination [of the Indonesians]."[7] Nor could slavery be abolished "until a higher order of general civilization will permit amelioration of their fate."[8] Jan Pieterszoon Coen, one of the founders of Dutch colonialism, put it plainly: "May not a man in Europe do what he likes with his cattle? Even so does the master here do with his men, for everywhere, these with all that belongs to them are as much the property of the master, as are brute beasts in the Netherlands."[9] Throughout the seventeenth and eighteenth centuries, however, VOC control over the East Indies was never quite complete or stable, as it faced increasingly belligerent local rulers, as well as peasant revolts and rebellions, particularly in Java and Sumatra.[10] Gradually, however, the Dutch began to rely on the rigid social hierarchies of the indigenous societies to administer the territories, relying on the *bupatis,* or aristocratic elites. They thus helped bolster the aristocracies of the islands and turned a blind eye to their customary authority over their subjects. Furthermore, the Dutch faced opposition to their hegemony in the region from the British, who were "the most powerful naval and commercial force in the Malay-Indonesian area."[11]

The Birth of Indonesian Nationalism

In the early twentieth century, the Netherlands government, which had now taken over the administration of the East Indies from the VOC, adopted a so-called Ethical Policy. Liberal critiques of colonialism had gained ground in Europe, at least since the publication, in 1860, of a novel titled *Max Havelaar,* written by a former colonial official, Eduard Douwes Dekker, under the pseudonym "Multatuli." *Max Havelaar*'s exposé of the oppressive and corrupt colonial regime was influential enough that it is sometimes considered the first literary expression of modern Indonesian anti-colonial nationalism. As Ricklefs argues, however, "the liberals faced a dilemma, for they wanted to be rid of the *cultuurstelsel* ["culture system," or plantation economy] but not of the profits which Dutchmen gained from Java."[12] Convinced that the best way to profit from their control of this vast territory was through education and the raising of living standards, the better to shift the economy toward a modernized capitalism, Dutch administrators gradually began to introduce some social and political reforms. For all the rhetoric of the Ethical Policy, however, the vast majority of their colonial subjects lived miserable lives, exploited both by the Dutch and by local elites. Thus, as late as 1920, for instance, the number of Indonesian students enrolled in secondary education was alarmingly minuscule: a mere seventy-eight out of a total population of over forty-eight million![13] In 1930, the literacy rate of adult Indonesians was at a shocking 7.4 percent, while in some areas like Bali and Lombok, it was lower still.[14]

Nevertheless, the Ethical Policy saw the rise of a new educated elite and, consequently, of a modern Indonesian nationalism. Indeed, the future leader of the Indonesian struggle for independence and undoubtedly the most important political figure in Indonesia's recent history, Achmed Sukarno, was very much a product of this period. Sukarno was educated at one of the few secondary schools that admitted Indonesian natives, the Hogere Burger School in Surabaya. The early years of the twentieth century witnessed the growth of the first nationalist association, the Budi Utomo ("Pure Endeavor"), which later morphed into the first truly mass organization of Indonesians, the Sarekat Islam (SI).

Sarekat Islam was formed initially by Javanese merchants in defense of their interests against the growing power of Chinese merchants, whom the Dutch favored. At first, the SI gatherings were local spaces for traders and businessmen to seek redress for what they saw as unfair treatment at the hands of the Dutch. Soon, however, these local SI branches became a magnet for ordinary Indonesians—peasants, workers, and the poor—to voice their grievances as well. The formation of the SI and the founding, in 1920, of the Communist Party of Indonesia (known by its Indonesian initials, PKI) opened up a new era in Indonesian history, that of mass anticolonial nationalism.

Indonesian nationalism was from the beginning a heterogeneous combination of different, sometimes contradictory, tendencies. As early as 1918, the SI newspaper, *Utusan Hindia,* proclaimed: "We are pursuing not independence but freedom. We call for the freedom of mankind, for wiping out the difference between rich and poor."[15] Similarly, Sukarno developed a style and rhetoric of leadership that allowed him to deftly straddle different ideological currents. Thus, in 1921, he declared in an *Utusan Hindia* article: "Socialism, communism, incarnations of Vishnu Murti, awaken everywhere! Abolish capitalism, propped up by the imperialism that is its slave! God grant Islam the strength that it may succeed."[16] On the basis of this ideological "synthesis" of nationalism, Islam, and Marxism, Sukarno founded the Partai Nasional Indonesia (Indonesian National Party), or PNI, which was to be the main vehicle for anticolonial agitation in the years to come. This mélange of religion and Marxism would remain the hallmark of Sukarno's political strategy up until his death in 1970.

The Japanese Occupation

The Dutch, however, faced no serious challenge to their rule during the first decades of the twentieth century; rather, it was the Japanese army that broke the back of the Dutch colonialists during the Second World War. When the imperialist rivalries of the Great Powers exploded in the form of the Second World War, the Asia-Pacific region became the stage

of a contest between the United States, on the one hand, and
Japan on the other. None of the European powers had much
of a role to play in the Pacific war, and they were rapidly de-
feated by advancing Japanese forces. The Japanese had already captured the imagination of the colonized nations of
East and Southeast Asia by defeating Russia earlier in the
century; now, as the European colonies fell one by one to the
Japanese onslaught, many were ready to welcome the latter
as liberators. Any illusions to this end were, nevertheless,
soon destroyed, as the Japanese forces proved to be just as
brutal and oppressive toward the Indonesians, and in some
instances more so, than the Dutch. The Japanese occupied
Indonesia for three and a half years, from 1942 to 1945.
During this time, however, they paradoxically set the stage
for a future Indonesian revolt that would ultimately lead to
independence and self-rule. As Ricklefs argues:

> Japanese policy towards Indonesians had two priorities:
> to wipe out Western influences among them and to mo-
> bilize them in the interests of Japanese victory. The
> Japanese, like the Dutch, intended to control Indonesia
> for their own interests. They faced many of the same
> problems as the Dutch and employed many of the same
> solutions (indeed, Dutch colonial law remained in force
> except where it conflicted with Japanese military law).
> But the Japanese, in the midst of an enormous war re-
> quiring maximum utilization of resources, decided to
> control through mobilization ... rather than by imposing
> an orderly quiet. As the war progressed, their increasingly
> frenetic efforts to mobilize Indonesians laid the ground-
> work for the Revolution which was to follow.[17]

The United States, of course, won the war. Japan was
crushed, with the firebombing of Tokyo and the dropping of

atom bombs on Hiroshima and Nagasaki. On August 15, 1945, the Japanese surrendered. The United States began its years-long occupation of Japan, which it used as a base to project its power throughout the Pacific, from Korea to Vietnam to Indonesia itself. It has often been suggested that the bombing of Hiroshima and Nagasaki was not the final shot of the Second World War but the opening salvo of the Cold War. The whole world was now carved up into two huge empires, one headed up by the United States, the other by the Soviet Union.

Independence, Sukarno, and the PKI

Two days after the Japanese defeat on August 17, Sukarno read out the Indonesian declaration of independence at a small ceremony outside his house. Meanwhile, the victorious Allies shamelessly rushed to reclaim their colonies as the Japanese troops were leaving. The Dutch troops who returned to stake their claim to Indonesia were aided by British commandos and American forces (although by 1947 the United States began to push within the UN for a Dutch withdrawal and for Indonesian independence[18]). Recolonization, however, was impossible, as the Indonesians launched a revolutionary war of independence and finally drove out the Dutch in 1948.

Several political currents that had been driven underground in the recent past now reemerged, stronger than before, including the PKI, the Socialist Party, and the PNI. Sukarno by this time had established an unquestionable dominance over the progressive forces in the country and en-

joyed a degree of popular support that few postcolonial
rulers have had. In part, this is attributable to his remarkable
ability to fuse together left-minded reformism, anti-imperialism, and religious sentiments in his own unique brand of political ideology. By 1960, he had given it a label, Nasakom,
derived from the Indonesian terms for nationalism, religion,
and communism. Thus he called for a "national front"
against imperialism.

The most dramatic development in the postindependence decades was the rise to prominence of the PKI as the
third-largest communist party in the world, after those of
Russia and China. Throughout the Cold War years, both the
Russians and the Chinese had enormous influence over the
PKI and other mass communist parties that had emerged in
Asia. There were differences in the tactics that each of them
advocated in the struggle against imperialism—Maoism
tended to appear more "militant" and left-wing, while Stalin-
ism tended to appear more "moderate." But while their tactics may have been different, their strategy was ultimately
geared toward the same end—consolidating strong national
states, with top-down, bureaucratic regimes in control. In
other words, they tried to remake Asia in their own image.

On the other hand, the U.S. strategy during the Cold
War was one of "containment," which meant putting down
any resistance that threatened to bring the former colonies
into the Russian or Chinese orbit. Asia thus bore the brunt
of the Cold War more heavily than any other region in the
world. Two major wars in Korea and in Vietnam alone ac-
counted for some five million deaths, with the United States

testing its newly acquired weapons of mass destruction, na-
palm and Agent Orange. The struggles of the Left, particularly in Indonesia and Vietnam, were thus shaped by the
Cold War more than anything else. Revolutionaries around
the region were urged, by both Russia and China (although
differently), to support their national bourgeoisies against
Western imperialism. Strengthening the national state
against imperialist aggression meant, however, that the over-
throw of their own ruling classes would have to wait for
some later stage. This strategy was to prove disastrous in a
number of instances, especially in Indonesia.

As the PKI grew in influence, it attracted an impressive
following among workers, peasants, students, and intellectuals. Thus Pramoedya Ananta Toer, while not a card-holding
member of the Party, found himself on the board of the
PKI's cultural organization, LEKRA, which at its height
claimed a membership of some one hundred thousand. By
the early 1960s, the PKI had a membership of some two
million and had become the largest and most organized political force in the country. However, the PKI, in keeping
with the approach advocated by Moscow and Beijing, called
for a "united national front" that would include "the working class, the peasantry, the petty bourgeoisie and the national bourgeoisie." The tasks of the Party, the PKI insisted,
were to bring about "not socialist, but democratic reforms."[19]
In so doing, however, the PKI risked losing its independence, as its leader, Aidit, himself recognized when he wrote
that while "unity with the national bourgeoisie is getting
closer and closer ... the alliance of workers and peasants is

not strong.... There is danger of losing the Party's independ-ent character, the danger of its merging itself with the bour-geoisie." In the very next sentence of this document, how-ever, Aidit characteristically went on to insist that "the Party must preserve this united front with all its might."[20]

Meanwhile, Sukarno continued his balancing act be-tween the various political and ideological currents that were jostling for power in postindependence Indonesia: the reli-gious groups, the Communists, and the army. In a speech delivered on June 1, 1945, Sukarno laid out his doctrine of Pancasila ("Five Principles"),* which codified in philosophi-cal terms the political strategy that he hoped would allow him to stay in control of an increasingly unstable political milieu. Pancasila would, in the coming years, become the of-ficial ideology of Indonesian nationalism. The five principles were: "belief in God, nationalism, humanitarianism, social justice and democracy."[21] Furthermore, notwithstanding his overtures to the PKI and his lip service to Marxism, Sukarno's Pancasila was also based on *gotong rojong,* or mu-tual cooperation, "between the rich and the poor, between the Moslem and the Christian."[22]

By 1957, Sukarno set out to establish what he referred to as "Guided Democracy," which reflected a deepening of the crises that this balancing act was meant to dampen. During the period of Guided Democracy, the army began to play an increasingly central role in administration and politics. Rick-lefs argues that in the following years "Sukarno had little power of his own and was obliged to manipulate, threaten

* See Glossary

and cajole other powerful men. Intrigue and conspiracy became the common fare of politics. The political elite became a complex of cliques around influential men."[23] In retrospect, therefore, it becomes all too clear that the PKI's desire to maintain its alliance with Sukarno, on the one hand, and to stay true to its revolutionary principles, on the other, was doomed to failure.

The 1965 Coup and Suharto's Reign

As John Pilger points out, "Sukarno had relied on the communists as a counterweight to the army, which, having been trained by the Japanese during the Second World War, basked in its own mythology as guardian of the nation."[24] The PKI, in turn, had developed a trusting relationship with the charismatic Sukarno, even as it adopted revolutionary goals and rhetoric in its propaganda. The contradictory character of the PKI's politics would ultimately lead to its downfall. On October 1, 1965, a failed coup attempt by some army officers was blamed on the PKI. "Before the day was out," reports Rex Mortimer, "the head of the army's strategic command, General Suharto, had put the rebel forces to flight and brought the capital under control."[25] Mortimer goes on to describe the aftermath of this failed coup:

> [T]he capital was in a state of shock. Rumors and lurid reports relating to the affair swept the city…. Although Sukarno insisted on devising a political solution to the crisis, and forbade punitive action, the army moved on its own initiative to ban PKI activities, arrest Communists and suspects, and suspend members of the party holding official positions…. A ruthless campaign of extermination of Communists and alleged Communists

was inaugurated in Central Java and quickly spread to East Java and other provinces.[26]

The bloodbath that followed is estimated to have resulted in the massacre of an estimated one to three million Communists, radicals, and activists. According to a report by the CIA, "In terms of the numbers killed, the massacres rank as one of the worst mass murders of the twentieth century;"[27] nevertheless, there is reason to believe that the CIA was itself responsible for "spreading the myth that Suharto and the military had saved the nation's honor from an attempted coup by the … PKI, whose 'carnage' had caused a 'spontaneous, popular revulsion.'"[28] According to Joseph Lazarsky, the deputy CIA station chief in Jakarta, "We were getting a good account in Jakarta of who was being picked up. The army had a 'shooting list' of about 4,000 or 5,000 people. They didn't have enough goon squads to zap them all, and some individuals were valuable for interrogation. The infrastructure [of the PKI] was zapped almost immediately. We knew what they were doing…. Suharto and his advisers said, if you keep them alive, you have to feed them."[29]

Tragically, the PKI disintegrated without much of a struggle to defend itself. Mortimer explains: "A dispersed and shattered leadership seems to have lost all capacity to rally the party or cope with the decimation of its ranks. Sticking to the last to the hope that Sukarno would pull their irons out of the fire, the leaders went into hiding and became to all intents and purposes deactivated."[30]

The conflagration that engulfed the nation also changed Pramoedya's life forever. On October 13, he was arrested by an armed mob and taken first to the Army Strategic Reserve Command Post and then to the Regional Military Command Post in Jakarta. His library was ransacked, and "thousands of books, documents, and years of accumulated research" were piled up and burnt to ashes.[31] Thus, at the age of forty-one, Pramoedya was imprisoned and banished to Buru, a remote, isolated island, where he spent the next fourteen years in exile. As Willem Samuels tells us, even in these conditions of severe repression and deprivation, "he somehow managed to write and, with the help of sympathetic missionaries and visitors, smuggle from the island five historical novels [four of which form the famous "Buru Quartet"–NR], a play, and an estimated thousand pages of scattered papers."[32]

The New Order military dictatorship of General Suharto, perhaps one of the most brutally repressive the world has seen, lasted for more than thirty years, thanks in large measure to the benevolence of the Western powers. Suharto's Indonesia was long considered by Western capitalists and their institutions, such as the IMF and World Bank, as a "model pupil," so that, as Pilger puts it, "globalization in Asia was conceived in Indonesia's bloodbath."[33] During this time, the World Bank handed out more than $30 billion to Suharto's regime, some 20 to 30 percent of which went into the coffers of Suharto and his cronies, according to a secret internal World Bank report.[34] The U.S., British, and Australian governments lavished praise on Suharto's dictatorship for bringing "stability" to Indonesia, with Margaret Thatcher referring to him as "one of our very best and most valuable friends."

Suharto's crimes during his ascension to power were many, but were soon to be rivaled by his brutal invasion and annexation of the tiny neighboring island of East Timor in 1975. As is now well known, the Indonesian military invaded this country of six hundred thousand within hours of the departure of visiting U.S. president Gerald Ford and Secretary of State Henry Kissinger. Despite the fact that, in the following five years alone, the Indonesian military is estimated to have killed nearly a third of the population of this former Portuguese colony, the major powers, including Australia, the United States, Britain, and France continued to supply the Indonesian military with arms, money, and training.[35] Southeast Asia expert Benedict Anderson reports that

> 90 percent of the weapons used for the invasion came from the USA. Although their use outside Indonesia was expressly prohibited by a 1958 American-Indonesian agreement, Washington, well informed by the CIA of Jakarta's preparations for invasion, turned a blind eye to the violation.[36]

When the regime desperately required Bronco aircraft for aerial bombardment of Timorese resistance fighters, "the Carter administration secretly supplied them, while lying to Congress and the public that an embargo on military equipment was in place."[37] It is this history of U.S. duplicity and connivance with the Indonesian dictatorship that fuels Pramoedya's rage against the American government.

The Western powers' self-assured confidence in the stability of the Suharto regime received a rude shock in May 1998, when, a few weeks after he was sworn in for a seventh consecutive term as president, Suharto's brutal rule finally came to an end. A mass uprising, led primarily by students, overthrew his regime on the heels of a terrible economic crisis.[38] On May 12, snipers shot and killed four students at Trisakti University. The Australian socialist Tom O'Lincoln describes what happened next:

> Students began to drift into the streets. Here they were joined by workers, the unemployed and the poor. The police marched up and street fighting began; I tasted tear gas for the first time since 1969. Around Atmajaya University in the heart of the city, office workers left their desks and came into the streets to express their support for the students. By nightfall, riots were spreading and the following day saw Jakarta in flames. Few corners of greater Jakarta were untouched. Some neighborhoods looked like war zones. Finally the dictatorship cracked.[39]

This revolt was the latest chapter in a long history of courageous struggles waged by ordinary Indonesians against oppression and tyranny. Nevertheless, there is yet much to be done, and Pramoedya's words in the pages of this book ring with the sense of urgency that one has come to expect from a writer and activist who has lived through some of the most volatile moments in Indonesia's history.

O'Lincoln continues: "But the May unrest was only partly an uprising. Yes, there were sensational actions directed against the government. But it also involved race riots, rapes and apolitical mass looting, and a significant amount of it was orchestrated." Thus the *reformasi* movement was contradictory; on the one hand, it represented the outpouring of accumulated anger against the Suharto regime, while on the other it failed to put forward a liberatory alternative to the domination of Indonesian elites. The anti-Chinese riots, the numerous accounts of women being gang-raped while hysterical crowds cheered, and the chaos and looting were symptoms of a movement that had little conception of a way forward. Consequently, early characterizations of the upsurge as heading toward a liberatory revolution appear in retrospect to have been astoundingly mistaken and misleading. Consider, for instance, that the current Indonesian president, Susilo Bambang Yudhoyono, is a former army general and is married to the daughter of General Wibowo, who played a leading role in the 1965 coup and subsequent massacres. The army, it appears, has not loosened its grip on the Indonesian state, and corruption in high places is as rampant as before, and probably more conspicuous. Thus it is not surprising to find, in the conversations that follow, Pramoedya's outrage against the bankruptcy of contemporary Indonesian politics and culture. As he suggests, the New Order regime has merely recycled itself and, absent the renewal of a politics of liberation, especially among Indonesia's youth, will remain in power, bleeding Indonesia's social, economic, and cultural spheres of life and vitality.

1. K. M. Panikkar, *Asia and Western Dominance* (New Delhi: George Allen & Unwin, 1959), 21.

2. Quoted in Panikkar, 21.

3. Ibid., 22.

4. Ibid., 87.

5. Ibid., 40.

6. M. C. Ricklefs, *A History of Modern Indonesia Since c. 1300*, 2nd ed. (Stanford, CA: Stanford University Press, 1993), 26.

7. Panikkar, 86.

8. Ibid.

9. Ibid.

10. See Ricklefs, 94ff.

11. Ibid., 142.

12. Ibid., 124.

13. Bernard Dahm, *Sukarno and the Struggle for Indonesian Independence* (Ithaca, N.Y.: Cornell University Press, 1969), 29.

14. Ricklefs, 160.

15. Dahm, 37.

16. Quoted in Dahm, 39.

17. Ricklefs, 201.

18. The United States in the postwar period painted itself as a champion of "democracy" and "self-determination," the better to strip its imperial rivals of their colonial possessions and thus strengthen the political, economic, and military supremacy that it had gained as a result of the war.

19. Rex Mortimer, *Indonesian Communism Under Sukarno: Ideology and Politics, 1959–1965,* (Ithaca, N.Y.: Cornell University Press, 1974), 46.

20. Ibid., 47–48.

21. Ricklefs, 209.

22. George McTurnan Kahin, *Nationalism and Revolution in Indonesia* (Ithaca, N.Y.: Cornell University Press, 1952), 126.

23. Ricklefs, 257.

24. John Pilger, *The New Rulers of the World* (New York: Verso, 2002), 26.

25. Mortimer, 388.

26. Mortimer, 388–90.

27. Quoted in Pilger, 25.

28. Ibid., 25–26.

29. Quoted in Pilger, 30.

30. Mortimer, 390.

31. Willem Samuels, "Introduction" to Pramoedya Ananta Toer, *The Mute's Soliloquy: A Memoir* (New York: Penguin, 1999), xix.

32. Ibid., xxi.

33. Pilger, 28.

34. Ibid., 20.

35. For an excellent account of the Indonesian occupation of East Timor, see Constâncio Pinto and Matthew Jardine, *East Timor's Unfinished Struggle: Inside the Timorese Resistance* (Boston: South End Press, 1997).

36. Benedict Anderson, *The Spectre of Comparisons: Nationalism, Southeast Asia and the World* (New York: Verso, 1998), 133.

37. Ibid.

38. For an overview of the process that led to the downfall of Suharto's regime, see Anthony Arnove, "Indonesia: Crisis and Revolt," *International Socialist Review* 5 (Fall 1998), and Tom O'Lincoln, "Indonesia: The Rhythm of Revolt," *International Socialist Review* 32 (November–December 2003). Available online at www.isreview.org/issues/32/indonesia1.shtml.

39. Tom O'Lincoln, "Indonesia: The Rhythm of Revolt."

Prologue

Meeting in Jakarta

Andre Vltchek

The twentieth century was an almost uninterrupted orgy of terror and violence, deceit and betrayal. Men and women on all continents learned that "a lie repeated a thousand times becomes the truth," that brutal occupation can be described as an act of liberation, and that a massacre of millions of innocent people can be defended by rulers of mighty and not so mighty nations as an advancement of humanism, civilization, and national interests.

Millions of men and women vanished in crematoria and concentration camps, on battlefields, or in the rubble of their bombed cities.

However, the twentieth century will not be remembered only for its brutality. In the midst of plunder and chaos, it also gave birth to extraordinary men and women who stood tall and, against all odds, defended the defenseless, the victims of governments and dictatorships: people who opposed demagoguery, militarism, and selfish economic interests with the two most powerful tools of resistance known to humankind: knowledge and truth.

Some died in the process; others suffered but survived. Many became icons for independence and resistance movements. They were not prophets or gurus. They were brave but not fanatical. As Albert Camus wrote in the unforgettable final chapter of *The Plague,* "Unable to become saints, they became doctors."

While entire continents were being plundered and innocent people exterminated or thrown into prisons, these men and women of principle were tirelessly identifying the symptoms of insanity, diagnosing the illness, and searching for the cure.

They were countering lies with simple words of reason, damaging myths with facts, fanaticism with truth. Some faced the madness with sarcastic smiles on their lips, others with tense expressions on their faces. Some rebelled and defended reason and truth with mailed fists; others raised their barely audible voices, which nevertheless made inroads into the minds of millions of people all over the world.

They were born in Europe and the Americas, in Africa and Asia, in every corner of the world. Most were raised by parents who were themselves victims, but many were the sons and daughters of the victimizers. Whatever their origin, the message was invariably universal and based on a single principle: all men and women are equal, regardless of their color or race, their nationality or gender, or their status and material possessions.

Indonesia, an enormous archipelago country made up of

diverse states, ethnic groups, cultures, and languages unified only after World War II, was previously controlled and exploited by colonial powers for centuries. After an honorable start to self-determination and twenty short years of genuine independence, it was plunged into the terror of military dictatorship after the 1965 coup.

Teachers were killed, film studios and theaters closed down, the Chinese language and almost all symbols of Chinese culture outlawed. Hundreds of thousands, possibly millions, of people lost their lives: Communists, progressives, members of ethnic minorities, atheists. Political, ethnic, and religious intolerance asserted their grip on power in this unfortunate country.

People's ability to argue, to question, and to compare disappeared. Creativity was crushed or simply discredited. Diversity was discouraged. Foreign travel became possible only for economic and political elites who were profiting from the "New" and "post-New" Orders.

Eventually Indonesia experienced social collapse. The great majority of its people now live in despicable conditions, most of them with no safe drinking water, many without electricity, more than half surviving on less than two dollars a day.

Truth was rarely allowed to surface; artists became complacent, and the media censored themselves.

During these forty years, a soft-spoken man from central Java wrote countless books, trying to define the essence and history of his young and suffering nation. He wrote in prisons, in camps, and under house arrest. He wrote in "internal exile," outraged and horrified about the state of the world behind his windows. Many of his books were burnt, and those that survived were banned. "It was my personal challenge to the dictatorship," he said later. All his books had one common theme and message: "Colonialism and imperialism—external and internal—are always wrong. The elites that enrich themselves by plundering their own people are immoral. In order to keep his dignity, a man has to fight injustice."

In a country so young and so troubled, where history had been distorted and corrupted, where unity was based more on Javanese lust for power and geographical considerations than on common ideals and culture, it is hardly surprising that the loudest voice of moral resistance attempting to unite the nation against terror and injustice should be that of the county's greatest writer, Pramoedya Ananta Toer.

*   *   *

We first met Pram, as he is known in Indonesia, in his house in East Jakarta in December 2003. At the time, we were preparing to shoot a long documentary film, *Terlena— The Breaking of a Nation,* about the murder and imprisonment of Indonesian intellectuals after the 1965 U.S.-sponsored military coup. Our objective was to convince Pram, arguably the foremost living Southeast Asian novelist, to participate in the project. After all, he had dedicated his life to defining the essence of this enormous fledgling nation, criticizing its negative aspects in the process. It was he who had denounced Suharto's regime as "morally corrupt." Pram spent decades in jails and concentration camps and under house arrest. His manuscripts were burned by the regime and his books banned in Indonesia until 1999.

We arrived at his house accompanied by two young Indonesian journalists, both excited about meeting the great master of Indonesian letters; both very anxious, repeating that Pram "has a reputation of being extremely impatient, explosive and even arrogant."

We had to wait for at least half an hour. During that time, Pram's brother appeared. He refused to speak English, but then, with a knowing expression, he addressed me in Russian: "Of course, as an American you don't speak a word of Russian," he said. "I'm wondering what the heck you're doing here."

"I came to convince your brother to participate in a documentary film about the events of 1965," I answered in fluent Russian, a response that left him gasping for air. He gave me a big smile, sat down, and indicated that the ice was broken. "Then everything is fine," he responded. "Should I go out and get some vodka?" I had to decline his kind offer: it was still too early in the morning.

Pram appeared suddenly, accompanied by his wife and several relatives. He was frail and unshaven and smoked his clove cigarettes like a chimney, one after another.

He could hardly hear, so questions had to be screamed directly into his ear. I was sweating liberally as the sun climbed steadily, beating mercilessly on the roof and the walls of the house. As in most dwellings in Java, there were no air conditioners.

Pram asked several questions, and we got involved in a conversation about the books of Noam Chomsky, about *Z Magazine*, and the World Social Forum. He asked me to convey my greetings and thanks to Chomsky: "for all that he has done to help to uncover the truth about Indonesia's past." He then asked how old Chomsky was. "Seventy-three? That's good: he's still a young man compared to me," he said, laughing.

There was no hint of arrogance in his behavior. If anything, he was warm-hearted, sarcastic, laughing, and joking, his face constantly changing and expressive. Sometimes there were long pauses in our conversation, as he withdrew into the world of his memories. During these moments he would touch his unshaven face with the hand holding the cigarette, his eyes concentrating on some point on the opposite wall.

When I asked him about the Indonesian press, his tone of voice changed. "I have become so impatient with them. They come here and ask me all those stupid questions.... They don't know what they are talking about.... I really cannot deal with them."

He happily accepted our invitation to participate in the film and invited us to his main dwelling, an isolated house in a remote suburb of Jakarta called Bojong Gede, Depok.

After a while, his facial expression changed again. He suddenly looked very old and vulnerable: "Sometimes I feel very isolated. I'm living in my own world, and it's like being in internal exile. I'm wondering if people still care about what I really think."

I told him that they did and still do, that probably hundreds of thousands of men and women all over the world would like to read his thoughts, especially now, after his long years of literary silence.

"I'm never going to write anything, anymore," he said. "I can't: I simply can't write. My last book will be just a collection of some old letters that I sent, years ago, to several important political and cultural figures."

Without much thinking I said, "So why don't we write a book together? I will be working in Indonesia for several months, maybe years. Why don't we try to re-create the past, together? I am not burdened by the details; we can search together for the essence of what has occurred in your country. Why don't you say all that you always wanted to say and never did?"

To my surprise, he didn't hesitate at all. "Let's do it, then," he agreed. He wondered aloud whether he and I, an American, were "good for each other"; hardly surprising considering that it was the United States that had brought down Sukarno and destroyed Indonesia, after all!

Before leaving his house, he confessed that later that afternoon he intended to travel to east Java by bus. "I want to see Indonesia again." As we stood up to shake hands, he almost fainted from exhaustion. I had to carry him to his relatives, and was shocked by the fragility of his body.

Back in the crowded center of Jakarta, we were overwhelmed by the weight of the enormous responsibility that was falling upon us. It was going to be we who would be bringing the last words and thoughts of the author of *The Girl from the Coast* and the "Buru Quartet" to the world; of one of the founders of Indonesia and a committed opponent of Suharto's terror.

All doubts disappeared two months later when we sat with Pram in his dark living room around a large circular table. Two recorders were running, and the endless smoke curling from his cigarettes was coloring the air and caressing the ceiling. He hardly looked at us. Sometimes we weren't sure whether he was aware of our presence: he seemed to accept our questions as if they were coming from some abstract, undefined source. His mind was traveling in the far remote past, to a different Indonesia, a country that both of us were too young to remember. We were in his Indonesia, an imaginary country forever lost.

Those days of work were difficult and often painful. Pram would get tired easily. Often he would repeat the same thought several times. He would get angry and frustrated remembering the past. Sometimes there were tears in his eyes.

It seemed that all his hopes for Indonesia had collapsed. One day he declared that Dutch and Japanese colonialism had been better than the current ruthless plunder by the Indonesian elites. I wanted to make sure that I understood correctly: this was hardly a statement one would expect from one of the founders of the nation. Or from a man who despises colonialism! But Pram insisted on what he had said: "Javanism" and Javanese colonialism had been much more brutal to the people inhabiting this enormous archipelago than had foreign colonial rule.

He drank endless cups of tea and smoked incessantly.

He refused to be labeled. Is he a Marxist? "No, I'm a

Pramist," he answered in a determined voice.

He doesn't believe in religion (although religion is the only thing even he is afraid to criticize openly in Indonesia). He is not a member of any political party. Socialist Realism is the literary form closest to his heart. And the most compassionate social system in the world can be found not in Asia or the United States, but in today's secular Europe.

It was obvious that he wanted to speak, that he had to speak, and there we were, trying to help him to shed the burden of his accumulated knowledge and pain by asking the questions that had, for decades, been forbidden even to be asked.

He had fought for an independent Indonesia and had put tremendous effort into building it: as a writer, thinker, historian, and journalist. He had expressed his love for his country through labor and struggle, not through the empty words of a racist patriotism. He had admired Sukarno but when the Chinese minority had been threatened even under Sukarno's rule, he had preferred to go to jail rather than remain silent. When Indonesia collapsed in 1965, with the military unleashing terror and ordinary citizens participating in religious and ethnic cleansing, Pram—imprisoned in Buru Camp—wrote some of his greatest novels, attempting to preserve the essence and the spirit of the young independent nation.

Today in Indonesia, he is hardly known. He lives in total isolation, in his "internal exile." Forty years of the free market economy, omnipresent propaganda, and the destruction of culture and intellectualism have created a climate where

Pram's thoughts are too terrifying to those who prefer to hide from the truth. He is an invisible giant in a nation whose people have been beaten down—morally and intellectually.

But perhaps Indonesia will eventually change. Perhaps the fear will subside; questions will be asked again, people will stand up for their rights. When this happens, Indonesians will once again search their past for personalities on whose principles to rebuild this bruised land. Then Pram will become, once again, a native son as well as one of the fathers of the nation; a man of tremendous creativity, moral integrity, humanism, and bravery. His comeback will announce the revival of Indonesia.

Jakarta, October 28, 2005

* * *

Have you ever written specifically about the Indonesian dictatorship and the impact it had on you and on people close to you?

Only in my letters and notes, and sometimes in my books. These things come directly from inside, but I have never written about it directly, as a memory.

Have you ever published a book in the form of questions and answers?

No, this format has only been used in interviews with me— interviews for magazines and newspapers. Nevertheless, I really welcome your idea of creating such a book. However, I can foresee a problem about writing this book with you. You are an American. Indonesia collapsed mainly because of the United States. In the past, Indonesia had chosen its own way, the path of development advocated by President Sukarno. He was our true leader. However, what was the U.S. reaction? The then-President Eisenhower issued orders to depose our freely elected president! I know they still hate Sukarno in your country because he strongly denounced colonialism, imperialism, and capitalism, even though he was a colonial product himself. That makes me wonder if we are right for each other—to write this book together. On the other hand, when I was serving my time in prisons and camps, I was helped by American people.

But that's exactly why we want to write this book with you. We have to tell the truth about the past—and how it influenced the presence—to both your readers here and your readers in the West.

Yes, I agree. So, why don't we try to write this book? I have so much to say. I want to speak about the young generations and about the students who fought until Suharto was forced to resign. I want to speak about other times, the occasions when people were hunted down, killed, and dumped into the sea. I have no access to the media and no organization to support me. I am burning inside. You came here so we can talk, so now I can open up and bother you with all the frustrations and curses that have accumulated inside me over long decades.

Chapter One

Before 1965:
History, Colonialism,
and the Sukarno Years

Can you describe your personal vision for Indonesia during the struggle against colonialism? What were your expectations when you were fighting for independence from the Dutch and the Japanese?

I was raised in a left-wing nationalist family that opposed the colonial system. I was brought up in that kind of environment. We dreamed of an independent, democratic country. From the time I was a child, I was told I should fight for that. My beliefs have always leaned to the left, so I was never inclined to seek the path to power instead of following the needs of the people.

How difficult was it to unite an enormous country with many different cultures and dozens of different languages? Is it really united now?

In theory, from the very beginning the several nations of the region agreed to unite to form one large country—Indonesia. The only exceptions were some small countries still under Dutch rule, such as the Moluccas. In reality, it wasn't as straightforward as it appeared—each nation's aspirations and culture were different from those of the others.

The acute problem facing the new country was a lack of education—even a lack of understanding of what education should represent. Families discouraged individualism. Personal initiative and risk-taking didn't exist, except in Aceh. The result was a spirit of "groupism," where people were courageous only when they belonged to a group and only dared to fight when they were part of a group. Villages fought against villages, districts against districts, students against students: all because they lacked individualism and personality.

Long ago, it used to be different. As schoolchildren, we were often abused by students from more prestigious schools. When this led to fights, we would gather in a field and each group would select a representative who would do the fighting. The one who lost had to shake the hand of the winner. Even in Wayang, our traditional puppet theater, it was always so—each individual puppet stood his ground when fighting another.

For many years, I have been thinking: How did Indonesia become like this, this country that we see now? How could it have become so "groupist," so supine, so lacking in individuality and identity? This is one of the weaknesses of our country—an inadequacy that may lead to Indonesia's downfall!

In today's Indonesia, the family unit doesn't teach its children how to produce, only how to consume. The result is that people have forgotten how to produce because they don't produce anything anymore, and when they can't produce, they become corrupt and try to corrupt others. Indonesia is united now, but it's a unity based on the wrong principles.

Was there a concept of a united Indonesia at the very beginning?

The concept had already been defined by the young generation in the Sumpah Pemuda—"Oath of the Youth"*— in 1928: "One country, one nation, one language." That was the basic principle and, as I said, in Indonesia the young generation always stood at the vanguard. One of our greatest forgotten heroes of the past was Muhammad Yamin.

Although he was among those who created the concept, today's historians don't even mention his name.

What impact did colonialism have upon the nation's identity?

Westerners came looking for spices in what is now Indonesia in the sixteenth century. They called it "East India" or later the "Dutch Indies." They never considered this area to be an independent culture. Even the present name means "Islands of India." During the colonial era, the countries in the area never considered themselves as strong and independent nations. Instead, they acted like servants of the West, mainly because of Javanism, a cultural attitude that eventually

* See Glossary

spread over all of what we now call Indonesia. Java was the center of colonial administrative power, hence the overwhelming influence of Javanism.

From my personal experience, the impact of colonialism was that in the past, we—even I—felt inferior to people from the West. I only lost my inferiority complex in 1953, eight years after independence, because I was then living in Holland and had a Dutch girlfriend [*laughs*]. However, that's just my own history.

Was an inferiority complex a general feeling among Indonesians in those days?

I think so. What I felt wasn't exceptional.

What about Indonesians who had never traveled or lived abroad? Did they ever lose their inferiority complex?

Many never did. That's why many of our people feel admiration for anything that comes from abroad: they prefer foreign things rather than something local. What makes me sad is that such admiration includes the language: the more languages we speak, the prouder we are. It means that we have no personality—we don't appreciate what we are.

So colonialism taught people to respect and fear power?

No, that had always been deeply embedded in our Indonesian culture. Javanism had only one principle—obedience and loyalty to the superior. That's why we were ripe for colonization. Understanding Javanism is crucial for understanding what became of us after 1965. In fact, the topic is so important that I would like to talk about it at length later in this book.

How brutal were the Dutch during their colonial period? Did anything positive come from it?

Brutality was, no doubt, common during the colonial period. On the other hand, at least the Dutch introduced some sort of equality to our society, a notion previously unknown. We had no prior concepts of humanism and internationalism; those concepts were eventually embraced by Sukarno. We attempted to implement them in 1945, during and after independence—both were concepts originating outside Indonesia.

When you were living in the Netherlands, did you ever feel that Europeans understood how much wrong they had done to Indonesia and other colonized nations?

No, for them it was the spirit of the era and they didn't feel any guilt.

Did you experience any form of racism when you were in Europe?

Yes! When I lived in Holland, I always felt that Dutch people were lecturing me. Eventually I got fed up with it. No matter whom I talked to, I felt they always thought I needed to be lectured just because I came from a poor country. I didn't like having my inferiority complex constantly pushed down my throat.

According to many people who lived through these times, when the Japanese marched into Indonesia, Indonesians were told they were being liberated from the West. Many Indonesians welcomed them with open arms. Then the Japanese Imperial Army began committing atrocities and the struggle for independence erupted. Is this what really happened?

The words of the Japanese imperialists were, of course, very different to their deeds. The first truckload of Japanese soldiers that passed the front of my house was carrying Australian soldiers whose feet were chained. Another truck passed carrying dead bodies. Behind them were Japanese soldiers carrying Indonesian and Japanese flags. They distributed leaflets saying that Japan and Indonesia were united, on the same side, that Japan was like Indonesia's elder brother. They were greeted by joyful celebrations. However, let's not forget that in 1942 Japan was still on the winning side of the war.

By 1943, things had changed and they were on the defensive. At that point, everything changed: they had to fight along the full length of Indonesia's coastline with inadequate manpower. They began recruiting Indonesians, forcing them to join the army. It soon became obvious that they were no longer on the same side as the Indonesians. They also began taking food and crops from the farmers and introduced *romusha*—forced labor. About seven hundred thousand farmers were conscripted to build fortifications inside and outside Indonesia. Of those, approximately three hundred thousand died.

I regarded the Japanese invasion as wrong from the very beginning; I was always taught to see any form of colonialism as wrong. Nevertheless, you're right: it's an undeniable fact that most Indonesians accepted the Japanese invaders as liberators.

How different were the Dutch and the Japanese occupations?

The Dutch believed in a rule of law while the Japanese didn't. Within three days of landing in Java, almost all Japanese soldiers were raping local women. At the time, women painted their faces with coal dust so the soldiers wouldn't recognize them as women. Even old women were doing it; even grandmothers.

From the beginning of the invasion, there were some very strange moments. For example, the Japanese soldiers broke down the doors of Chinese shops and allowed the mob to loot freely, but three days later, almost all the looters were executed.

The only good thing to come from the Japanese occupation was an edict that Bahasa Indonesia was the only language allowed to be spoken. Immediately after the occupation, they banned all the languages of their enemies, including Dutch and English. Mainly because of this regulation, Bahasa Indonesia was able to develop. The Japanese even had a special committee translating and converting all foreign language phrases into Bahasa Indonesia.

When you say that the Dutch believed in the rule of law, wasn't there a different legal system applied for colonizers and colonized?

Yes, it was different, but both parties were still subject to at least some law. The Dutch were subject to different courts than those for local people. Furthermore, Dutch colonialism was aided by the presence of a Javanese nobility that didn't fall under anyone's jurisdiction—if a nobleman committed a crime, he was not punished. For him, the worst that could happen was exile.

In your novel, The Fugitive, *were you writing about your own experience during the Japanese occupation or was the story fictional?*

The book was inspired by actual events during the PETA* revolt against the Japanese.

How did you personally celebrate independence on August 17, 1945? What was the mood on the streets of Indonesian cities and villages during the declaration of independence?

Independence found me at the foot of Kelud Mountain, on the run after abandoning my job at the Domei Japanese news agency. I saw Indonesian recruits and PETA fighters from the Japanese army returning home carrying rice. I wondered what was happening, and they told me that Indonesia had declared independence two days earlier.

What was your reaction; how did you feel?

At first, I thought, "This is the fulfillment of my childhood dream!" I went straight to Surabaya, and from there I trav-

* See Glossary

eled to Blora and then to Jakarta. However, when I arrived in
Jakarta, fighting had already begun, this time against the
British. I joined young people from the neighborhood and
fought alongside them. The situation in Jakarta was tense:
whenever we heard a truck passing, we were ready to fight.

*So immediately after celebrating, you had to fight in order to
defend the newly independent nation.*

Yes. As soon as I arrived in Jakarta, I was aware of several
worrying and dangerous circumstances, including the arrival
of the British Royal Army, the presence of confused and
angry Japanese soldiers who had just lost the war but were
still armed, and Indonesians armed with Japanese weapons.
All three groups began looting, and there was constant fighting. The Indonesians were ready to fight, even without the
weapons.

During the first week, we—that is, myself and the
young people from Kemayoran—went to the Japanese compound, searching for arms. When we arrived, the Japanese
were just hanging around, calm and relaxed, showing no sign
of fear. I found it extremely strange. One of them said,
"What do you want? If you want to take our things, just take
them. Look, here, I have a letter." He showed us the letter: It
was from Sukarno. It stated that whoever read the letter had
an obligation to spare these people's lives. "Whatever you do,
don't kill these people," it said.

It seemed that a group of Japanese had helped Sukarno
declare independence. Because of the letter, we were unable
to collect any weapons. Immediately after our visit, the

Japanese soldiers left the compound and we took over. As it turned out, we were attacked by Australian troops a week later and, as we had no weapons with which to defend ourselves, we were unable to stay there. So, these are my personal recollections of the days after the declaration of independence.

Was there a feeling among your comrades that it was the beginning of history, or was it all such a mess that you had no time to even think about it?

We all felt drunk from the joy that came from independence. We were full of emotion, unable to think about anything else.

At this time, were you hoping that Indonesia would become an egalitarian, socialist state?

Sukarno was considered an enemy by almost all Western capitalist countries. He was avowedly anticapitalist, but initially national unity was the most important goal. Yes, above all we were thinking about national unity. Later, after Suharto's coup turned everything upside down, the country's direction was no longer clear.

When did you meet Sukarno for the first time?

Immediately after the war. I saw Sukarno on several occasions but never in private. The first time we met was when I offered support for his idea of "guided democracy" on behalf of Indonesian artists. The second time I went to the presidential palace, where he was drinking coffee with his ministers. I don't remember all that was said on that occasion, but I recall that I suggested to Sukarno that he should commission and erect a statue of Multatuli,* but he refused. I still believe that Multatuli should be recognized as an Indonesian national hero, because he was the person who told the Indonesian people the truth about colonialism. Before him, under the spell of Javanism, Indonesians didn't even realize that they had been colonized.

What can you say about Sukarno? He's well known as a statesman, but how was he on a personal level?

I always respected him. I agreed with his views, especially when it came to his ideas about national character building. They were extraordinarily visionary, but, after the 1965 coup, nobody wanted to talk about them anymore. He had profound insight into Indonesia. He knew about the history of his country. During his era, Indonesia was regarded as an enemy of many Western countries, because Indonesia stood against colonialism, against imperialism, and against capitalism. That's why I was, and still am, absolutely supportive of him. At the time, I also supported him when he fought against *Manikebu.* *

Nevertheless, I had no particular personal experience of him. Actually, Sukarno didn't know much about me. Once we met and he addressed me with the words "Brother Pram, you are a Muslim scholar, right?" [*Laughs.*] It showed that he knew nothing about me.

* See Glossary

By the way, do you have any religion yourself?

I only believe in myself, and, as time passes, I believe in myself more and more. I spent thirty-four years in prisons, camps, and house arrest and God never helped me. People come to God to beg—in fact, praying is begging.

Economically, Indonesia was poor at independence; lately, it has become one of the poorest nations in Southeast Asia. How different was the lot of simple people during the Sukarno era and now?

Today's poor people have been impoverished by the elites. Before independence, they were robbed by the colonizers; now they are robbed by the elites. Poverty existed under Sukarno because our country was besieged by Western powers. All Western countries were antagonistic toward us, and the domestic economy hadn't developed. During Suharto's era, it was totally different: he allowed Western money and Western investment to enter the country. Every time an amount of Western capital was invested in Indonesia, much more had to be squeezed from us in return, because capitalism only cares about higher and higher returns.

During Sukarno's rule, almost everybody was equally poor. If there was corruption at that time, only a small amount of money was involved. Present-day corruption involves billions and billons of dollars.

Pram, was there a feeling of hope during those decades before 1965—when Sukarno was in power?

Yes, under Sukarno there was hope, but then everything was destroyed by the coup that brought Suharto to power, and Sukarno's supporters were eliminated. Before that, there was hope: Sukarno was truly loved by the majority of Indonesians.

Under President Sukarno, Indonesia became a highly respected country able to make a significant impact upon the world. For instance, it was one of the founding members of the Non-Aligned Movement. Sukarno was a champion of the idea of unity between developing nations, something that is still considered a valuable concept of a possible future realignment of the world's political and economic blocs. Did Indonesian people understand those concepts at that time? Did they support them?

Yes, Indonesia was respected by other nations. It was like a lighthouse of hope for other developing nations in Asia and Africa. Sukarno was a great orator who never hesitated to talk to the masses through radio and television. Practically everybody in this country knew about the concepts he was advocating.

However, although the majority of the people loved him, there was some opposition. Liberal intellectuals, especially those who advocated extended civil liberties, disapproved of his approach. At the time, Sukarno was pushing full force for the guided democracy, so there were bound to be intellectual clashes. Groups that opposed him mostly united around the Socialist Party of Indonesia. They included public and media figures such as Syahrir,* Muchtar Lubis, and Rosihan Anwar.

* See Glossary

*What was the idea behind the Non-Aligned Movement, from
an Indonesian perspective?*

The idea of a non-aligned movement was necessary and important in order to fight imperialism. At that time, almost all
African and Asian countries were still controlled by imperialist countries. The policies of Sukarno helped in the liberation struggles of those countries. Singapore and Malaysia
won their independence because of Sukarno's involvement.

*Was the independence of colonized countries the only goal of the
world Non-Aligned Movement at that time?*

The goal was to win independence and then build democracy in those countries.

*Even before 1965, you were regarded as the greatest Indonesian
writer. How did you feel about living in the so-called guided democracy that was implemented by Sukarno's government? Did
you have any disputes with the system?*

I have always been regarded as an enemy by all Indonesian
governments, even by Sukarno [*laughs*]. Under Sukarno I
spent almost a year in prison, because I wrote *Hoakiau* in Indonesia. At that time, the Chinese community was not allowed to trade in this country. People of Chinese origin were
forced out of their villages, and some were even killed. I was
against it. That's why I was sent to prison in 1960.

*Still, looking back at the Sukarno era, do you feel that the gen-
eral direction in which the country was developing was correct?*

The general direction was correct, but I didn't agree with some elements, including discriminatory regulations against the Chinese community. These were actually designed by the military—the aim was to create tension and thus cut off ties between the People's Republic of China and Indonesia.

What was Sukarno's approach to the military? Could he have prevented the 1965 coup with a different approach, like reducing the size of the military?

Sukarno had no weapons; he was just a politician. The real power was concentrated in the hands of the military. There was nothing Sukarno could have done, because there were two centers of power. Those who toppled Sukarno were members of the army.

Were there strong ties between the Indonesian military on the one hand and the United States and other Western powers on the other before the 1965 coup?

Yes, those ties existed, of course.

Were there any predictions, any fears that there could be intervention from the West—any military coup—before 1965?

No, there was no suspicion at all. That's why, when it happened in 1965, everybody was in shock. It wasn't just shock: nobody had a clue about what was really going on. Even now, nobody knows for sure what happened, because everything was covered up. There are even discrepancies about how many people died after the coup.

What was the cultural climate during the Sukarno era? Was the main emphasis on local culture or was it on internationalism?

Mainly on local culture. For example, in music Sukarno was against trends coming from the United States. LEKRA was trying to promote local culture. Some of the local cultural movements that LEKRA tried to promote are still in existence today. The *ketoprak, lenong,* and *ludruk* traditional theater forms were elevated from street theater to large, nationally significant venues, and performances were broadcast on radio and television.

Many intellectuals from foreign countries voiced doubts about the cultural policy promoted by Sukarno, particularly about those elements that were supposed to define our culture under the name of Nasakom: nationalism, religion, and communism. They were skeptical that these elements could coexist, but they didn't understand that it wasn't about uniting the three doctrines—it was about creating the revolutionary spirit necessary to fight against imperialism.

Chapter Two

The 1965 Coup

How were you informed about the coup?

I found out from the radio. I was astonished, because the official version spoke about the PKI (Communist Party of Indonesia) being the instigator of the coup. Only later did I realize that it was the military itself. The main accusation spoke of the PKI trying to depose Sukarno, an obviously unrealistic version because the PKI was the main supporter of Sukarno. I was confused by the whole situation and kept thinking about it for months thereafter.

Forty years after the coup, there are two competing theories about what happened. The official version, put forward by Suharto, the Indonesian military, and the United States, was that the Communist Party was responsible for triggering the coup by kidnapping and murdering seven high-ranking military officers. Other historians suggest that the coup was actually car-

ried out by the pro-Suharto faction of the military and backed by the United States and other Western powers. What are your thoughts on this subject?

Of course, the main goal of the West was to depose Sukarno because of his three principles: anticolonialism, anti-imperialism, anticapitalism. There was friction in the military, which was divided into supporters of Sukarno and supporters of Suharto, whose goal was to grab power. It was a coup. One faction in the military was used to kill six generals and one army officer—an act that later triggered mass slaughter by Suharto's supporters. The victims were Communists, Chinese, and all supporters of Sukarno. So this is what happened: the military and Suharto staged the coup and then accused others of staging it, eventually killing two million people. Do you understand? They killed two million people as "revenge" for something they had done themselves!

There is a parallel in our Javanese past—the history of Kebo Ijo, who was ordered by Ken Arok to kill Tunggul Ametung. After Tunggul Ametung was murdered, Ken Arok came to power and ordered Kebo Ijo to be executed. So, as you can see, there is a pattern in our history.

Those who killed the six generals and one officer between September 30 and October 1, 1965—did they have any connections with the Communist Party?

At that time, the PKI was a legal political party, so the possibility of connections can't be dismissed, but I'm not aware of them. If they did, it was only on an individual level. Regardless of that, the coup had nothing to do with the Communist Party, but with a faction in the military that had been manipulated by, and was supportive of, the policy of the United States.

So the coup was not the work of the Communist Party but of elements in the Indonesian military that had been manipulated and influenced by the United States?

Yes.

The coup was followed by unimaginable brutality. How is it possible that the whole country stood aside during the massacres or directly participated in the slaughter? The great majority of Indonesians did nothing to stop the coup, to confront the military, to defend the principles on which Indonesia was supposed to be built, or to protect millions of helpless victims.

Simply because of fear! Because two million people were killed so quickly, a culture of fear was born: people were scared even to mention the name of the PKI.

Did the army really have such tight control of the country?

In reality, the military was in control of the country after the revolution, after independence. Even civil servants obeyed the military rather than their superiors. In this respect, nothing has changed from then until now. After the coup, the military and Suharto's political party, Golkar*—an organization with many civil servants in its ranks—created what is

* See Glossary

known as "New Order"—Orde Baru. Before the coup, the position of the army was not institutionalized: under New Order, it was incorporated into the body politic.

What was happening on the streets after the coup? There were massacres in provincial cities and villages, but what was the atmosphere on the streets of Jakarta?

There was total silence. People were petrified and had no idea about what was really happening. The military was arresting people everywhere without charges, randomly. The rivers were red with blood, but people didn't understand why! The river Brantas was clogged with dead bodies, but I only heard about it—I didn't see it personally, being already in prison. People were kept in the dark—they only knew that six generals and one army officer supportive of Sukarno had been killed during the night between September 30 and October 1, 1965. The people butchered by the military ranged from Sukarno supporters to members of the PKI. Although I was there when it started, I didn't witness what happened over the entire episode because I was arrested on October 13, two weeks later.

How many people were killed after the coup?

According to Sudomo,* the number was two million. If we were to go to Sudomo now, he probably wouldn't dare to repeat what he said. He holds no position now. Indonesia is bizarre: people are only daring when they have power. How-

* See Glossary

ever, most of the killing was done by those under the command of [General] Sarwo Edhie Wibowo, who, at one point, proudly admitted that his men managed to kill three million people, and he was only talking about the victims in Java.

Theoretically, Sukarno was still in charge—he was president—even after the coup, at least for some time. Why didn't he try to fight Suharto? Why didn't he order his supporters to stage an armed rebellion against the usurper?

Sukarno didn't fight Suharto because he wanted to avoid a full-scale civil war. Of course, the lack of resistance led to the total destruction of everything that he stood for.

Later, after all the plunder and the massacres, the intellectuals of Indonesia didn't dare to revolt: they stayed put and kept their heads down.

How bad was the military and government oppression after the coup?

The military and Golkar eliminated most of Sukarno's supporters and wiped out any opposition. In the main, they targeted Communists, but not only them. They also went after religious leaders and nationalists: those were either killed or sent to concentration camps, such as Buru. Between two and three million people were murdered. To give you an example, in Blora, the relatively small city in East Java where I was born, they managed to kill three thousand people.

At least the Blora massacre will be documented in a book that will be published this year.

On October 13, 1965, you were arrested. After your arrest, where were you taken?

They took me just about everywhere: to the CPM [military police] compound, to Kodam-5 [headquarters of the military], to Bukit Duri Prison, and to Tangerang Prison. For four years, I was moved from one place to another. Until I was transferred to the Buru Island concentration camp, where I spent ten years, I was tightly confined.

Can you imagine how I felt when everything was taken away from me? My wife and children had to stay with different people, to move from house to house. You can talk to her. She will tell you all about the hardships of that time, not to mention how she had to feed me because we were given hardly anything to eat in prison. Once, six people died from hunger in a single day!

What can you say about your arrest? How many people came to take you away? What were the charges? What did they say when they arrived?

Before my arrest, a mob attacked my house. I don't know if they were soldiers or civilians because their faces were covered, but they were throwing stones at my house. Every time I turned on the lights at the alley, they would back off, but returned immediately when it became dark again. I guessed that the mob consisted of people I knew, people who didn't want me to recognize their faces. I yelled at them, "This is not the way to fight, cowards! I'm also a fighter! Let me see your leader. What do you want? If you dare, come here and face me!" but nobody took up the challenge.

They continued throwing huge stones at my house, using sarongs as a launcher, until the front door began to give way. By that time, I was already bleeding. Even my legs were bleeding, but I was still standing in front of my front door, ready to confront them, my Japanese sword in hand. Then, suddenly, machine-gun fire erupted, "Ra-tah-tah-tah-tah!" and the mob froze. Then the armed forces arrived. They knocked at my door, so I opened it. I saw an entire platoon of soldiers. One of them said, "Mister, please don't fight the people," so I replied, "These are not people; it's just a mob."

Immediately after that, on October 13, 1965, I was arrested and everything that I possessed was confiscated. They took everything I was wearing, including my wristwatch. Up to now, they haven't returned what was removed, even thirty-eight years later. Even my house was confiscated and never returned.

I was taken away by truck and hit several times with a gun until I almost lost consciousness.

When they were arresting me, they kept saying "Let's go, Mr. Pram, we're going to save you!" That's the first time I ever heard arrest described as "being saved."

At the time, my wife was giving birth somewhere else. A neighbor told her what was happening to me. She rushed home but was unable to enter. She witnessed the burning of my eight manuscripts and all my documents. My entire library went up in flames, too. Burning manuscripts is something that can never be forgiven! Burning books can only be described as evil. The soldiers' act was proof of the degradation of their culture, of their vandalism: the antithesis of the creative process of writing, one of the main symbols of culture.

Before all of this happened, a friend, my assistant at *Bintang Timur* daily, came rushing to my house and said to me: "Brother Pram, terrible things are happening everywhere. I think you will fall victim to those events, too, because you are one of the leaders of the people." He told me what had happened to his neighbors—first the mob attacked them and destroyed their house. Later, they heard automatic machine-gun fire, and then the military arrived and arrested them. So, as you can see, what happened to me was very similar to what was happening to many others. My friend suggested that I should try to escape, to run away, but I thought, "Where would I go? This is my house and I am going to defend it." Ultimately, though, I couldn't fight an entire army platoon by myself.

Did they explain why they were arresting you?

They actually never said that they were arresting me. They kept repeating that they were "rescuing" me. That was a novel word for me! So, when they took me away, I carried my portable typewriter with me to be able to continue my work on the next sequence of my novel *The Girl from the Coast.* I took the entire unfinished manuscript of the third part of the novel. The manuscript of the second volume was destroyed in front of me!

At that time, I had several jobs: I was working as an adviser to a pencil factory. When people there realized that things were getting out of control, they brought me some money—three months' salary. I also worked as a professor at the university, and the same thing happened—I was given three months' salary in advance. That was just before my arrest, so I had the money with me. It was all taken, confiscated together with the other things. As I'd lost everything, I couldn't help my family.

Did they beat you in detention? Did they torture you? What kind of questions were they asking? What did they do to you?

In detention, I was neither beaten nor tortured. On one occasion, I had my face slapped by a corporal. He was asking me stupid questions, so I asked him, "What is your rank? How dare you ask me these questions?" The result was that he lost his temper and slapped me.

As for their questions, they just kept asking for my name, my address, over and over again.

As I said before, I wasn't ill-treated physically, but all my belongings were confiscated and all my papers and manuscripts were burned. Afterwards, my books were banned. I'm sure that all this was part of a very well-planned strategy.

Were any written depositions made?

No. There was no official interrogation and no deposition. I just disappeared!

Only after many years, after I had been released from Buru Camp and was under house arrest in 1988, three prosecutors from the Supreme Court came to question me. They were the first to make any deposition—they actually made two. I demanded a trial, and they all agreed. I demanded that I was to be represented by a lawyer from a neutral country who knew about communism. I insisted on this because I was certain that, if there were to be a trial, the judges and prosecutors would know absolutely nothing about the topic. However, my trial never took place.

By then your fame as a writer had spread worldwide. Did you get any preferential treatment in the prisons and camps? Many people died in detention, but you survived.

Not too special treatment, but I got moral support from all over the world. I got almost the same treatment as any other prisoner, but my monitoring was more rigorous. I was monitored even if I had to walk fifty meters. About surviving, I should mention something. Apparently, at one stage, there was an order to assassinate me, but the commander of the camp didn't dare to execute me. By then, there was already substantial international pressure.

So after being arrested and until your final release, you never returned home?

Exactly! I didn't return home until my release from Buru.

How did they transfer you to Buru concentration camp? Were you flown there, or did they put you on a ship?

We were put on a train from Jakarta to Nusakambangan, and from there we had to sail to Buru on a ship.

Who were the prisoners on Buru Island?

They were all men from all levels of Indonesian society.

If I understand correctly, when you arrived there in 1969, Buru was still a relatively small camp and only grew larger in the early seventies. How many prisoners were there when you arrived, and what was the highest number reached?

The first group consisted of five hundred people, and I was among them. At that time, there were no roads in the north of Buru Island, just a few in the south. Consequently, the first prisoners had to build over 170 kilometers of roads. Later, they brought many more prisoners: the number eventually swelled to fourteen thousand.

How were the conditions in the camp?

From what I understood, the camp was supposed to comply with certain specifications, such as concrete foundations and strong wooden beams. The reality was very different: the walls and roofs of our barracks were simply made of leaves. The entire area was fenced with barbed wire. All prisoners had to work in the fields.

What were you expected to do there?

I had to dig ditches, work on the irrigation system, build roads, and work on the rice fields. Eventually, I decided to treat this forced labor as a sport. Maybe, if I hadn't been sent to Buru, I would be dead by now, because what I did before was only reading, typing, and smoking. In Buru, I grew bigger and stronger.

Were prisoners tortured? Many of them died in detention, didn't they?

Yes, they were not only tortured but also killed. Later, I wrote about it in my book *Nyanyi Sunyi Seorang Bisu* (*The Mute's Soliloquy*). I wasn't tortured, probably because my whereabouts were monitored by the outside world. As for the other prisoners, there was a small hut built specifically for torture and killing, far from the place where I lived. My place was more toward the center of the island, but the hut was near the port. Once I saw a political prisoner forced to run, chased by a horse-driven carriage. When the prisoner couldn't run any longer, they ran him over with the carriage. I saw this happen with my own eyes. Being beaten up in the camp was considered quite normal.

To give some examples of life in the camp: In order to survive, some prisoners possessed farm animals and caged birds. One prisoner kept losing a chicken each day. He was very annoyed and eventually began searching for the person stealing his birds. One day he emptied the cage, hid the chickens, and replaced them with buffalo dung. What he didn't realize was that the thieves were from the military. On the next occasion when they came to steal his chickens, they only found shit. On the following morning, we were all summoned and asked who owned the cage. When they found out, he was brutally beaten in front of all of us.

Another example: One of my friends in Buru designed

and built a small fishpond, but he kept losing his fish. In this case, he knew that the military was involved in stealing them. When the soldiers found out that he had been monitoring their actions, they shot him on the spot. He died.

We were not allowed to read in the camp, but one friend of mine kept some bits of newspapers in his place. When the military found out, they tied him up and, two days later, we found his corpse floating on the surface of the river.

Other acquaintances worked in the rice field. They ate their lunch in the hut where they kept fertilizer. The fertilizer was in the form of a white powder, so when the military appeared, they assumed it was sugar. One soldier put the stuff in his mouth and instantly puked. All those in the hut were then mercilessly beaten. Again, the military accused them of deception.

Once I came close to being shot myself, but a friend of mine knocked the soldier's gun butt before he could fire. The reason they wanted to kill me was my clothes. When we were sent to Buru, each prisoner was allowed to bring only two sets of clothes. Since we had to work in the fields every day, my clothes eventually decomposed. One had to have at least some spare clothes for sleeping. When my clothes turned to rags, I put on shorts made of plastic sacks. When the military saw me, they screamed that I was insulting Eastern culture by wearing such stuff. They were really going to shoot me just because of that!

One thing is certain: if I hadn't been monitored by the international community, I would be dead by now.

People were killed. Some were executed for trying to escape and others for many other reasons. How many people died this way in Buru Camp?

From the two hundred people who died there, more than thirty were killed. Maybe I was wrong with the numbers, but I reported it like that in *Nyanyi Sunyi Seorang Bisu* (*The Mute's Soliloquy*). It has already been translated into English, Spanish, and Portuguese.

At some point, you were allowed to write your books in Buru Camp. There you wrote your most famous series of novels, called the "Buru Quartet." Were you provided with paper and pencils? Were there any restrictions on how many pages you were allowed to write each day?

I was allowed to write because of the pressure from outside. One day, in 1973, General Soemitro came to see me, carrying an order from Suharto. Soemitro said that from then on I was allowed to write. I had to find my own paper: I got it from the Catholic Church. Nevertheless, from my experience as a political prisoner, I knew that authorities would eventually try to confiscate my work, so I typed several copies of my manuscripts. One copy was distributed among my fellow prisoners, and one copy was given to the church and later smuggled out of Buru and forwarded to Europe, the United States, or Australia. In the end, I was right. Before leaving Buru, they confiscated all my manuscripts. They also confiscated my personal letter from Suharto.

Letter from Suharto?

Yes. He wrote to me, saying that to make mistakes is human, but a man has to have courage to improve [*laughs*].

Is it true that the Catholic Church played a positive role in Buru and that many prisoners converted from Islam to Catholicism?

Correct. Muslims sent to Buru by the government kept lecturing us about our wrongdoings. I remember clearly one sentence they kept repeating: "Serves you right! Now you are like a dog with its tail between its legs." The Islamic people always swore at us and ridiculed us whenever they arrived in Buru. All of them! However, while Muslims kept insulting us, Christians offered some support. They gave us clothes and spectacles. That's why many people decided to convert to Catholicism and Protestantism.

Were prisoners allowed to convert to other "officially recognized" religions freely?

They had to convert secretly. As the government offered no help with churches, prisoners had to build them with their own hands.

In 1979, Suharto's regime finally decided to dismantle the camp. Where were you taken after Buru?

I was among the last prisoners to be released, but as the time to return home approached, we were told that we were not

going to be set free. The authorities threatened to send us to
Nusakambangan, another prison, but there was such a
strong outcry from the international community that they
had to transfer us to Magelang.

We sailed from Buru and, once in Java, they put us on
buses to Magelang. Later, they transported us to Semarang,
where we were paraded before foreign diplomats, while officials kept promising that soon we'd all be released. From Semarang, we traveled to Cipinang Prison in Jakarta. That's
where they finally released us, but it didn't mean that we
were really free—we still had to report to the local military
authorities once a week. Two years later, it became once a
month and, in 1992, I issued a statement saying that I refused to report anymore. Since then, I have been visited once
a week by an intelligence officer.

How did it feel to be back home?

I felt the same. Each injustice has to be fought against, even
if it is only in one's heart, and I did fight.

In what condition did you find your family?

Despite everything they had to go through, my family was
still better off than those of other prisoners, mainly thanks to
the international support and solidarity they received. In addition, my wife had established her own small business selling food. While I was in prison, the neighbors avoided my
family because they were too scared to be seen anywhere near
them. However, my wife's family accepted the situation, of-

fering and providing help. At school, my children were treated decently by their teachers, but that's mainly because, by then, I was already known as a writer.

And your neighbors? How did they treat your family during your imprisonment and how did they react to your return?

My neighbors reacted with understandable fear. They tried to avoid me, as they had tried to avoid my family before. In general, the family members of the victims were alienated by society: people didn't want to have anything to do with them.

After your return home, were you able to come to terms with the past?

I still suffer from nightmares, even now. I'm very happy if a single night goes by without them. My nightmares take different forms. Sometimes I'm being chased by the military. In others, I'm being tortured. Softer forms of nightmares are about forced labor. These things never really go away.

How difficult was it to reintegrate? When you talked to your friends and family, could they understand what you had been through?

I really didn't have to explain anything to my friends and my family. They already knew before I came back from different information sources.

You were forced to leave your life and sub-exist in camps and prisons. When you came back to the very different society created by Suharto's dictatorship, what impact did it have on you? Were you shocked by the changes?

I wasn't surprised at all. I wasn't shocked. I knew it would be like that after those terrible events. Indonesians, especially the elites, don't want to learn anything from history. I returned to a country that had lost its way.

How was your health when you were released?

[*Laughs*] Actually, I was very healthy, much healthier than before my arrest. I was big, strong, and had the body of a wrestler. I weighed seventy kilograms. If I had to chop wood, I was able to hold my ax with only one hand, but later, in 2000, I lost all my strength after a stroke.

Chapter Three

Culture and "Javanism"

You often speak about Javanism as if it were the most devastating aspect of Indonesian culture. Can you describe Javanism?

Javanism is an unthinking loyalty and obedience to a superior—to any superior—and eventually leads to fascism. Let's call it Javanese fascism—that's the system that had blossomed in Suharto's era.

What exactly do you mean by "Javanese fascism"?

It's the same as Javanism: blind obedience and loyalty to superiors, and no respect for the rest of the people. That's why Java was occupied by foreign powers for centuries. The Javanese elites collaborated with the colonial powers that were looking for spices. People didn't dare to challenge the elites, nor the colonizers. From the earliest days of colonialism, the elites were bribed by the colonial powers and Java fell into the hands of the enemies without a single battle. Our superiors never had any morals. Since then, nothing has changed. Nowadays, looters from all over the world are plundering our oceans, but the armed forces that are supposed to fight foreign invasions are only fighting their own people, something that people like me experienced personally!

Even the Javanese language is hierarchical: it's designed to glorify superiors. When it's translated to politics, it turns to fascism. It tolerates no opposition.

Can you offer some examples?

All right, let me give you an example of Javanism. I experienced Japanese occupation. The Japanese understood our mentality—they knew about Javanism and used it to their advantage. The Japanese gave orders to the local administration, including the local village chiefs, but never stripped them of their own authority. Those chiefs then voluntarily sent villagers, hundreds of thousands of them, to *romushal,* forced labor, inside and outside Indonesia. Many died or never returned to their hometowns. Despite what was happening, people continued to obey the orders of village chiefs—orders that came from the Japanese. I saw it all with my own eyes. This is Javanism: an unwritten law that says that orders from superiors should always be obeyed.

Another example: In the sixteenth century, when crews of Dutch ships were sent to loot our raw materials, the village chiefs were given gold and silver as compensation so that they wouldn't protest. The villagers didn't dare to protest either, because of their deep respect for higher authority. Javanism! The whole nation was plundered and the only peo-

ple to benefit were the foreign invaders and those who belonged to local elites. Something similar is happening now.

*Of the world's great cultures, the Indonesian culture is still one
of the least known. Why is it so introverted, and why does it
have no influence outside its boundaries?*

A great Indonesian culture? I disagree! Indonesian culture is
poor. Of what does it really consist? A real Indonesian culture had not yet been born. What we know as Indonesian
culture is just something we can describe as local or provincial cultures. What is Indonesian culture? There is some literature, true. That can be considered as Indonesian culture,
because it uses the Indonesian language. What else is there?
There are only some local cultural forms, like Balinese dancing. Every province has some folklore, especially Aceh. But
culture…?

For the last hundred years, Java controlled everything. In
my opinion, the young generation has to create a new culture and forget about the old stuff. It hurts to put it like that,
but it's true.

We were occupied for centuries, because our culture
couldn't match and surpass that of the occupiers, because it
couldn't fight them. Our values were low, too. Indonesians
constantly glorify their culture, but I keep asking, "What's
there to glorify?"

*Pram, you are probably the most outspoken critic of Javanese
culture. You have been critical of it both as a writer and as a
thinker. However, in your personal life, have you ever revolted*

against Javanism? Have you ever revolted against it in your own family circle, encouraging your family members to act differently from the rest of society ?

Sure! For example, I don't use the Javanese language at home. I refuse to use it, because the Javanese language uses a hierarchical structure that, as I said earlier, leads to Javanese fascism. To use the Javanese language gives me chills.

About my family! I taught my children and grandchildren about freedom. Now it's up to them what they make out of it. One thing that I have always demanded from them is that they take responsibility for their actions. That's all. One has to be brave to do that. I gave my children freedom and told them to be responsible for their own lives. That's why I always feel offended when my grandchildren keep asking me for money. I have never done anything like that in my entire life.

One of the negative results of me being imprisoned for fourteen years was that I was unable to educate my own children. I consider that my greatest loss. It's a mess. When I see my grandchildren asking for money, I feel that's one of the by-products of spending all those years in prison.

To change the culture, one has to be brave. Recently, I hosted a group of young people. I told them, "You, young generation! If you are not brave, you'll end up like cattle, just eating and multiplying."

When I was a child, I always rebelled against my father. Even if it wasn't always pronounced, I did it with my actions. I never revolted against my mother, though, because I deeply respected her. She was the one who made me like this. My mother used to say, "Don't ever beg. Learn how to be independent and always use your own strength. You have to study in Europe, and you have to graduate there." She pronounced these words even though, at that time, we were dirt poor. That's my mother. I always tried to put her words into action, and I continue to do so now. I have always respected her more than any other person in the world.

What happened to Indonesian culture after the coup, after all that bloodshed that followed 1965?

Since then, there really is nothing you can call Indonesian culture. There is only a downfall of the culture, total collapse. Even before the coup and the bloodshed, Indonesian culture was a chimera. Since the very beginning, it was never like that of China. For thousands of years, the Chinese wrote masterpieces and documented everything, while Indonesians only wrote about power and their royalty. Especially now, Indonesia has an extremely limited number of intellectuals. Almost every important work about Indonesia has been written by foreigners.

Two months ago in Yogyakarta, Djokopekik, a great Indonesian painter, told me that after the coup, every important artist in Indonesia was imprisoned or forced to leave. He said that cultural creativity was destroyed after 1965. Do you agree with him?

They were not arrested just because they were artists. Every supporter of Sukarno was arrested, and many were killed.

The regime probably didn't care much whether those people were artists or not. Artists who were not arrested accepted the new rules—New Order—and thus came under Suharto's control. Suharto is a very uneducated man: even his Javanese language is pathetic.

Is it true that there is in Indonesian culture a deeply ingrained necessity and desire to believe in something: in the family structure, in one of the officially recognized religions, in the leadership, in nationalism?

Families are not educated, so they can't educate their children. That's why the Javanese are not productive; all they know is how to consume. If one can't produce anything, he or she becomes a servant. There is no identity without production! Indonesia is a nation of manual workers, so one thing it exports well is people: it has become one of the largest exporters of cheap labor in the world. They can do only things that they are told to do and take orders from anyone who is willing to pay them. You can forget about creativity: creativity is something they lack absolutely, but creativity is not the first step. Before reaching it, they would first have to learn how to produce.

But, to answer your question, Indonesians still believe in myths. Rational thinking comes from abroad, and Indonesians are only beginning to learn about its existence. Our common people are still painfully backward. Compared to Malaysia, we are way behind. I see Indonesian thought in a constant process of rotting, and I can't do anything about it. I can influence things only when I'm invited to speak, and the last time I spoke in public, it was exactly on this topic: the low level of Indonesian culture. Even after I'd delivered my speech, the people in the auditorium still couldn't understand what I was talking about. They continue to believe that their culture is high. They keep glorifying it.

It seems that Indonesia's young generation is being indoctrinated by a vertical, inflexible, and extremely conservative family structure. Not to have one of the "official" religions is unthinkable; most of the people who would opt to leave religion would be excommunicated, even destroyed, by their own families and society. Do you suggest that young people should revolt against their families and religions?

To revolt or not to revolt, young people have to learn how to be rational, how to think. In my opinion, religion only teaches people how to beg, but maybe other people will feel insulted by my views. However, if they are saying that God is fair, can they show us where that fairness can be found in this world? They also say that God is omnipotent, but again I disagree, because I believe that everything on this earth depends on human effort. Better to depend on one's own strength than to expect something from above. People shouldn't act and think irrationally. They shouldn't have irrational expectations. Again, this is what I think and maybe religious people will be angry with me for pronouncing such words. However, in my lifetime, I have been robbed, imprisoned, and tormented for thirty-eight years. How could I not revolt against all that led to it?

If parents are not good, why should the children respect

them just because they are older? Children exist because their parents enjoyed the act of breeding. Here, words are always twisted: breeding is called love and begging is called praying.

How difficult is it to go against the mainstream in Indonesia? Religion introduced many negative aspects to Indonesian society, but nobody here dares to criticize it. Indonesians are kept from any books, articles, and films that oppose religion. They are not even allowed to read that the great majority of people in the developed world have lost all interest in religious teachings. Officially, 97 percent of Indonesians are religious. We haven't come across any criticism of religion in your books. Why?

To do it is so extremely difficult! Religion offers people dreams of heaven and many other things. On the other hand, when it comes to terrorism, the source is always religion. Look at the suicide bombers. They are willing to kill other people just because they have a different religion. They believe that such acts will bring them great rewards in another life. You can see how difficult it is to talk rationally to extremists. Religions say that the promise of heaven comes from God, but in reality, it was invented by people.

Do you regret that you never criticized religious indoctrination in your books, now that religion is increasingly gaining control of people's lives?

Once again, to do so would be extremely difficult in Indonesia. From a rational point of view, Indonesians still have the mentality of beggars: they always hope to get something from above without using their own abilities. Therefore, if one criticizes religion, one has to take on the whole society, and I was never strong enough to do that. Those who have their promise of heaven are sometimes brave enough to do just about anything as a group. Look at our local terrorists: when they are given death sentences, they just laugh!

Sometimes it seems that Indonesian people are afraid to think. Not just about religion, but about anything substantial. Any serious topic seems to be censored not just by the state, but by the society itself. Everything is discussed on a superficial level, as if there were a fear that thinking and analyzing could reveal the terrifying state of affairs in which Indonesians are now imprisoned.

Yes, and that's because this nation has refused to educate itself. Don't forget what formed Javanese culture: all concepts came from outside—nothing was passed on by our ancestors. Never forget that fact! Law, equality, humanism—all this is new to Indonesians. People here learned about humanism from the introduction of Pancasila.

When parents send their children to elementary schools, they are immediately squeezed for cash. It's the same when they send them to high school or university, but once they graduate, they become unemployed. And why's that? It's because our students aren't taught to be creative and productive. People are educated only on paper. The system produces a species of "warehouse scientists."

Our teachers aren't any better. I just read an article in a newspaper about a competition concerning rewriting Indonesian history. Both students and teachers participated, and guess who lost? The teachers! This clearly illustrates the local conditions, so don't expect any deep thoughts from them.

If things are so negative, is there a chance that some positive changes are on the horizon?

You shouldn't be asking me this question. Change is the obligation of the younger generation. Yes, it depends solely upon the young, but our young generation can't even come up with its own leader!

But this young generation grew up in a dictatorship, a despotic regime that used disinformation and brainwashing to strengthen its control. Isn't the current young generation in a much worse position than their earlier peers, who at least experienced some freedom and alternatives before 1965?

I agree, this is one of the main problems: the problems of the young generation! But on whom else can this nation rely? Indonesian history was always made by young people, ever since Sumpah Pemuda. At least they managed to bring down Suharto in recent history.

I keep telling them, "Your problem is that you are unable to find yourselves a leader!" I spoke frequently on this subject, asking young people to get together, mobilize, and launch a national youth congress so they could finally select a real leader, but, up to now, there has been no movement in that direction.

You mentioned Western rationalism and logic and Indonesian backwardness. Didn't this Western "rationalism and logic" lead to imperialism and colonialism, and even to supporting the 1965 coup in this country?

No, you are only selecting one negative result. There are positive things that one can say about rationalism and logic. Look at the opposite: Suharto didn't think rationally. He relied only on his instincts. I try to see it all dialectically.

Western colonialism brought some benefits. For example, the unity of Indonesia was created by the Dutch. We learned about administration and governance from the Dutch. We learned about the rule of law from the Dutch. We also learned about education from them. And what do we do with all that we learned? Education became a tool to apply pressure, to indoctrinate, and to extort money from students. This is happening from elementary schools all the way up to universities. Then, when the students graduate, many of them become unemployed. This is today's Indonesia!

Western colonial powers destroyed millions of lives and entire cultures in what is now known as Latin America. They destroyed nearly the entire continent of Africa and a huge part of Asia, including Indonesia, which was plundered and exploited by Dutch colonial administration.

That was the spirit of the era. During those times, colonialism couldn't be avoided. Nobody was able to fight or stop the exploitation of the southern part of the world by the North. It's nonsense to think that colonialism could have been stopped: the North was too powerful. These are all facts: this is how the spirit of those times really was. However, dialectically, this situation also brought benefits. We were able to learn about the West and learn from it. Indonesia was united by foreigners, not by local people.

But wasn't 1965 a typical example of what you call "Western rationalism"? The United States needed access to a cheap labor force and to the markets of Indonesia for its companies and geopolitical interests. It also aimed to destroy Sukarno's left-leaning government because it was becoming too influential in this region and beyond.

Yes, the strategy of the United States was to make the whole world its "dollar field." Sukarno opposed those designs, so they decided to get rid of him. It's an example of the downside of Western rationalism, of its negative impact on the world. Of course, there is a long tradition of negative colonialism in America itself. The settlers eventually destroyed most of the entire native population, and those who were left were stripped of their dignity and identity. While visiting the United States, one of the bizarre things I noticed was that all peoples of the world have their own restaurants there, except the indigenous Americans. The same goes for Australia, of course.

Wouldn't it be better and more natural for this part of the world to develop on its own, without interference from the West, without colonialism?

Then there would be no Indonesia. Local tribes would still be fighting each other. Today, we have almost no records of past battles: records came with the colonial powers. The Dutch colonialists were able to stop tribal fighting in what is now Indonesia. Due to that fact, the population increased, particularly on the island of Java. Law and a police force were introduced. Again, I'm trying to look at it dialectically. What was bad in the past has to be balanced against the positive results and vice versa.

Nevertheless, I definitely agree with you that the North was mainly interested in the natural resources of the South, not in helping its people.

So do you, the greatest Indonesian writer, really believe that this country lost something by gaining its independence?

Independence had to be gained, no doubt about it, but after gaining their independence, people refused to obey the law; they lost their fear. All I know is that today's Indonesians have no idea of what should be the concept upon which to build this country. People, and this includes our youth, just indulge in small talk, not how to achieve things. Now there is a movement here to trash rotten politicians, but all politicians here are now rotten!

Consequently, I have to say that even colonial government was better than what we have now. It's a very harsh thing to say, but look around you! One can't have respect for any of the current presidential candidates. None of them even understands the concept of Indonesia: maybe none of them has any individual achievements. All they can do is talk about nothing. There was no real election campaign, because no one had anything to say. To me, they are all clowns.

For example, although Indonesia's environment is being progressively ruined, none of the politicians or candidates is addressing the issue. Our forests are being plundered and our neighboring countries are profiting from it, but none of the candidates is willing to discuss it. They even allow Malaysian workers to enter our territory to do the logging while we just stand and watch! Our forests are being plundered, but nobody is held responsible.

So what can we expect from our leaders? Today's ruling Indonesian elites are behaving in the same way as the colonial powers, or even worse. All they care about is how they can squeeze money from the country for their own interests.

Returning to post-1965 Indonesia, there was at least some opposition or resistance in most of the former dictatorships, such as Argentina, Uruguay, Chile, and South Africa. How can it be that Indonesia lost somewhere between eight hundred thousand and three hundred thousand of its people without an armed struggle or resistance? Was it because of its culture, because of what you call Javanism?

How could we have had resisted? The real power was held by the army, with all administrative issues controlled by the Golkar Party. The fusion of those two elements was called Orde Baru, or New Order. It was so easy for them to kill people! The coup was followed by the slaughter of around two million people, so the population was petrified. Even intellectuals didn't dare oppose Suharto's New Order. The army and Golkar had their roots in *kaum priyayi* [the upper class and aristocracy] and kept records on everybody. All administrative power rested solely in the hands of Golkar, and the West supported Suharto's dictatorship. Practically everyone was too afraid even to speak, so people kept their mouths shut. Those who publicly denounced the atrocities, such as George Aditjondro,* were Indonesians living abroad, not those who stayed in the country.

This matter is also related to Javanism. Obedience to any power, to any superior: it all has roots in the Javanism, in the culture of Java. Indonesians are cowards. Up to now, no charges have been brought against Suharto. Even now, only a few lonely voices dare to address these issues! Ordinary Indonesians were too afraid: they just said yes to everything. Although some people knew how to fight, they weren't united, so they were unable to offer credible resistance.

The mass media had an enormous impact on the way the citizens of Indonesia regarded their own country and the world. How would you describe the mass media in this country? Do you think it is any more free now than before Suharto's downfall?

They are still like puppets manipulated by those in power. They serve the elites and the military. The situation is improving slightly: at least there are some free electronic media outlets, so the authorities can't just cover up things as they did in the past. An example is the case of Tomy Winata and

* See Glossary

Tempo weekly magazine, a libel issue that led to a much-publicized court case.*

Why is there no curiosity left in Indonesia? In almost all other dictatorships, educated people printed and smuggled books and periodicals that could throw light on their situation. In many totalitarian societies, people hungered for the truth and, as a result, often ended up better informed than their peers in democratic countries. Why didn't the same occur in Indonesia? Why is there almost no interest in the country's past, in its position in the world, in the political and social system, or in atrocities commited in East Timor, Aceh, and Papua?

I don't know how to answer this. From when I was a child, I always read newspapers in Bahasa Indonesia, in the Javanese language, and in Dutch. Now, even in my own family, my children and grandchildren don't read newspapers anymore. I can't understand it. Why don't they want to read the newspapers? Why are they only interested in trivia? They've lost the culture of reading and prefer watching television. I think that most Indonesian families are the same. They just glue themselves to the television. There is no hunger for knowledge.

Why are there so few good books available in the Indonesian language? People have to go to English-language bookstores to buy important works of contemporary thinkers and writers. Is it because only elites read books in this country, elites who understand English? Or is it because of the lack of good translators?

* See Glossary

Indonesians only became accustomed to reading after independence. Before that, they didn't read, apart from a few exceptions, of course. Since there is no long-standing tradition of reading, there's no tradition of writing or translating either. That's the problem! Now, even Malaysia is well ahead of us. Even though their population is much smaller, they produce more significant literary works than we do. As I mentioned earlier, Indonesians are not taught to produce!

Indonesian entrepreneurs are not interested in promoting literary works. Books are cheap here and are printed in small editions, so for them it's simply not a lucrative business. Translators are paid a pittance, so it's not an attractive job. In present-day Indonesia, there is little to support the development of literature. When I was still young, I had to write at least four articles a month in order to survive. Then I began writing for *Star Weekly* and I could easily live for a month from just one single piece. Writing is very hard in itself, but to earn anything from it is becoming even more difficult these days. Ideally, people should be able to live from their writing. As for me, I can live from it, but only because I am paid for my books published abroad.

Isn't there a danger that the Indonesian intellectual elite will become totally Anglicized, that it's going to divorce itself from its own language?

Of course! Indonesians are looking toward foreign countries. The further they travel, the more important they feel. Furthermore, the Indonesian language is a mess! Because the Japanese banned all the foreign languages spoken by their enemies, Bahasa Indonesia developed strongly during their occupation. The so-called Terminology Commission was created to translate all foreign technical terms to Indonesian, and it was obligatory to use the Indonesian language. Now people mix foreign languages with Indonesian, so it becomes banal and meaningless: "Let's go, happy-happy!" for instance. It's so different in other countries. Even in Germany all foreign words have to be translated to their national language.

Indonesians are simply stupid! Words are adopted from many foreign languages, including Arabic. The word *adil,* meaning "just," comes from Arabic, as do *adab* [culture] and *beradab* [civilized], not to mention *hukum,* which means "law," even though the concept of law itself comes from the West. Words in our language don't come from our own ancestors. People here think that if they utilize foreign words, they become more intellectual. What kind of intellectuality is that?

Is this the legacy of the Suharto years?

Suharto and his regime lacked any sort of idealism. That's why our culture degenerated into trivia and entertainment, and eventually became so incredibly shallow that a normal human brain could find nothing to digest. Everything became empty. Indonesians are force-fed with lies. Local television shows many heroes, but the reality is that this country was colonized for centuries, with almost no resistance. What kind of heroes do we have? Real heroes, people like Muhammad Yamin, Marko, and Tirto, who tried to bring progress to this nation, are never mentioned in our history books. After being bombarded for decades by this sort of "culture," Indonesia understands, and is in love with, only one thing: entertainment, and especially anything to do with bedrooms and breeding. All this was planned by the regime. It created this kind of culture so that the nation would stop thinking and thus be easier to govern. The post-1965 Indonesian society was constructed on two pillars: entertainment and fascist oppression.

Chapter Four

Writing

You are considered the greatest Indonesian writer of all times. Does your literary work have any impact on the nation?

There is a group of young people who call themselves "Pramists" [*laughs*]. It seems that the impact is sufficient: even Gus Dur, the former Indonesian President Abdurahman Wahid, said that my "Buru Quartet" could easily become his bible. Nevertheless, in this country, people keep writing about my personal life, not about my literary work. As a writer, I don't always exist. There are many books about Indonesian literature, but not one mentions my name.

I've documented everything that people in Indonesia and abroad have written about me. I've documented it and filed it each year. I've even drawn up some statistics: the total usually comes to between six hundred and a thousand pages a year. Part of my documentation has been accepted by the Library of Congress in the United States. Let me tell you how it happened.

Two years ago, some Islamic youth movements were looking for documents related to my work: they were determined to confiscate and destroy everything. Fortunately, they were saved by the United States Embassy, which allowed me to store the documents in its compound. When the situation calmed down, they returned them to me, but in the wrong order. I queried it, and they explained that while they had the documents in the embassy, they copied everything and sent it to the Library of Congress.

You write exclusively in Indonesian. No doubt, it's a beautiful language, but is it rich? Is it a good language for writing novels?

The Indonesian language is useless, especially when it's used by the mass media. Whenever it stumbles over some complex issue, it immediately switches to English. It's really limiting and has no character.

One language that I really admire is Japanese.

However, when it comes to my own writing, I find the Indonesian language quite adequate for my needs. When I can't find appropriate expressions in Indonesian, I borrow words from the Javanese language. What else can I do? I have to set an example, because the Language Commission has no influence and does nothing to reinforce rules and regulations regarding linguistic purity. During the Japanese occupation, the commission was alive and effective, because it was backed by a Japanese determination to outlaw the languages of their enemies. Now it's extremely passive.

People here attach almost no importance to the development of their language. I wrote a book about the history of the Indonesian language: unfortunately, they burned the manuscript during the dictatorship and I never managed to rewrite it. As you know, writing can't be repeated.

This is a nation of more than two hundred million people. Apart from you, are there any more writers, filmmakers, or other artists who can offer a strong moral voice to the nation, become a symbol of opposition?

No. The only young writer I can stomach enough to read his work, or at least five or seven pages of it, is Seno Gumira Ajidarma, but don't forget that he had been brought up abroad, in the United States. His thoughts are more democratic than those of the others. However, I can't stomach the older generation of Indonesian writers either. It doesn't mean that I'm being arrogant: it's just a fact.

All large nations, such as China, India, Russia, the United States, Brazil, and Japan, have countless renowned writers. Nigeria—a country with a similarly brutal and complex past as Indonesia—offers to the world literary giants like Soyinka, Achebe, and Habila, as well as daring new voices like those of Chimamanda Ngozi Adichie. Why is it that present-day Indonesia is not giving birth to any great novelists or poets? Why are you the only influential novelist that Indonesia has produced?

The situation here is different. The life experience of most Indonesian writers is different from mine. I spent all my life fighting. I first fought against the Japanese occupation and, later, on the side of Sukarno's revolution. I was deeply involved in "nation and character building." That's what is lacking now. Nobody even talks about the nation and building its character any more. Writers should feel a great obligation toward their nations: they can't just write whatever they like. I realized that from the very beginning, and that's what makes me different.

Is it religion, and a cult of obedience, that is stifling creativity?

Look, if I answer this question honestly, most of the people here will get very angry!

Eight of your valuable manuscripts were destroyed by the military. How traumatic was the experience?

It was acutely painful, very traumatic. I feel the pain until now. When I recall what happened, I still suffer, especially in the knowledge that I will never be able to rewrite those books. At the time, I was in prison, so there was nothing I could have done to save the manuscripts. Those books could have been published by now. When I was in prison, however, I was officially accused of being a Communist, and no publishing house in Indonesia dared to think of publishing any of my books.

Which manuscripts were destroyed?

A series on Kartini, an Indonesian national hero, including three books and a collection of Kartini's original writings. There was a book I wrote on the history of Indonesian language and two sequential volumes of *The Girl from the Coast*. Sorry, but right now I can't recall the eighth one.

How did you react?

It was really a character assassination: what they did to my books, they did to me. Now I just pity the people responsible—they only demonstrated the depths to which their culture had sunk. At the time, I took it as a challenge and continued writing in prison. My writing was my answer to them: by continuing, I showed that my culture was superior. That's how I fought them. I don't know how other people fought, but that's what I did. I was always taught how to fight, and it kept me alive! By now, my friends who were unable to fight are dead.

How did this experience affect your creative life? Are you angry about all those years spent in prisons and camps, about having your manuscripts burned by the regime?

I don't feel angry at all. I see it as an example of the debasement of my nation's culture. I use my writing to show that my culture is more advanced than that of others in Indonesia. I use my writing as a counterattack. I never give up, not even now. The communication gap between the others and me is sometimes too wide.

One day, I was summoned to the Supreme Court. The person who met me spoke continuously, but I understood nothing. After two hours, he started to make a little sense, and then said, "Mr. Pram, we are from the Supreme Court and we would like to ask you to change your views at least a little bit." My answer was "Those who made me like this were my own countrymen. If they want me to change just a little bit, they have to change a little bit, too. Moreover, after what I just told you, I'll not come again even if you try to summon me. If the Supreme Court needs me, it has to come to my house."

The first part of The Girl from the Coast *ended with your grandmother leaving the aristocrat's compound where she had been abused and humiliated. What was going to be the continuation of the story? What had you written in the second and third volumes of the novel?*

The story continued with the relationship between my grandmother and my mother and with my own personal testimonies.

The Girl from the Coast *is probably your most daring attempt so far to define Javanism. In a poetic and subdued manner, it exposes a cult of compliance and hierarchy.*

Yes, exactly. I tried to show that. I'm against the entire Javanese culture.

Despite the criticism, there was much love for and understanding of Java and its culture. Was it really intended just as a criticism, or was it also a tribute?

Do you really see it like that? From all that comprises Javanese culture, I love only *gamelan* music [*laughs*]. I don't even like Javanese dancing; I prefer flamenco [*laughs*].

Read outside Indonesia, The Girl from the Coast *doesn't appear to be only a critique of Indonesian or Javanese culture.*

But it is. All Javanese people know is how to work and to obey. They don't care if they are exploited and they don't care who exploits them: they just work. As a nation, ultimately they are dreaming one collective dream: how not to work at all. However, in the real world, they just keep working and working. The longer and harder they work, the more exploited they are.

I wrote about the life of Javanese people in my book *Tales from Blora,* although then I still didn't see the whole picture as I see it now. These days, I try to understand the broader picture. Then, I was just describing what I saw. By the way, as we speak, *Tales from Blora* is being published in the United States and *The Girl from the Coast* was published in Greek last month. That makes me happy.

While writing the "Buru Quartet," did you have an entire concept in your mind or were you working on each book separately? Had the idea to write it come to you in Buru?

Even before I was sent to Buru, I already had the concept: the groundwork for this series of novels had been very broad. One part was done by my students. Let me tell you a story about how it happened. One day, a professor from Leiden University paid me a visit and offered me an opportunity to lecture to classes at Res Publica University. I responded,

"How can I teach at a university if I never finished junior high school?" [*Laughs.*] Nevertheless, he insisted, and finally I felt I had no choice but to accept.

When I was faced with the class, I had no idea of what to teach or how to teach it. After a while, I came up with a solution. I asked each of my students to go through the old newspapers, starting with those from the beginning of the century, and to produce papers describing each period in our history. These papers gave me important guidance for the concept: that's how I gathered materials for the Quartet.

Using my students' notes, I was able to write *Sang Pemula* (*The Pioneer*). With the concept in my head and with all this material from my students, it was easy; all I had to do was sit down and type the book.

How do you physically write your books? Do you use a pen or a typewriter? How many times do you usually rewrite each manuscript?

I use a typewriter, and I never rewrite my manuscripts. That's the way I create: always a single attempt, and no rewriting. After my work is published, I never read it again. If I read it after writing it myself, there would always be a desire to change something in the text [*laughs*].

Of course, in Buru camp I had to use a pen.

How old were you when you decided to become a writer?

I started writing in 1947, because I needed to take care of my younger brothers and sisters. At that time, I had to write like mad in order to get some money. I didn't know how to do any other work, so I just wrote [*laughs*]. You could tell that I wrote in order to survive. From the beginning, it seemed that readers enjoyed my writing, so I chose to continue. By the way, some of my early work will be reprinted soon. I'm always glad when they reprint my old books, maybe because I can't write anymore. Who knows why? Maybe because I smoke too much? [*Laughs.*]

What were your writing habits? Did you write at night or during the day? Did you impose a schedule on yourself?

I never had any schedule and wrote whenever I felt like it. If I didn't feel like writing, I didn't do it—very simple. I don't impose forced labor on myself.

Are you disciplined? How many months or years did it take you, on average, to write one novel?

I'm not disciplined at all. I write whenever I want to, and that makes me feel free. That's why I've never disciplined myself when working on a novel. It all depends upon my mood, really. I never burdened myself with a schedule, so I can't answer your question about how long it takes to write, because it's always different, it varies from book to book.

What inspires you? How do you get yourself into a writing mood? Do you take a walk, do you smoke, do you drink coffee? Is it hard to get yourself to the table to start working on a book?

I get my inspiration from life. When something touches me

or outrages me, it fires my inspiration. Writing is always a fight: it's all about struggle! In all of my books, I promote the fighting spirit. I was raised to be a fighter.

Were you ever nominated for the Nobel Prize in Literature?

Sure, I was nominated almost every year. It's not surprising, because my books had already been translated into many languages. However, I never expected I would win that prize. If I were offered it, I would accept. Although if it happened now, I don't know if I could travel to receive it. I'm old now. I've just received an invitation to travel to Norway next month to receive their literary award, but I can't go because of my health.

Does the Nobel Prize mean anything to you, or do you consider it just a subjective, conservative, Eurocentric award?

It doesn't mean that much to me, and maybe that's why I'm not really expecting it. If you get an award like that, all it actually means is that your books will sell more copies. If I earned some money from that, I would use it to finish my encyclopedia project. I've already collected about four meters of material but still can't finish it. I try not to expect too much from the outside world. I learned to expect things only from myself. I never even asked for anything from my own parents.

Had you ever made an attempt to rewrite at least some of those books that were destroyed?

No. One can write a book only once. The surroundings and the mood one is submerged in during the writing can't be re-created.

Now, honestly, what are your true feelings towards the Javanese culture and society? We discussed this topic for many days, but I feel that there is still much you are keeping to yourself, highlighting only negative aspects of it. You were betrayed and suffered badly. Nevertheless, you're purely an Indonesian writer, after all. All that you write about is directly connected to Indonesia. Even when you speak about the worst aspects of its culture in its past and present, isn't it still a combination of pain and love that you feel toward it, or is it just pain and anger that's left?

When I experienced injustice, I didn't really feel angry because I realized that my personal culture was on a higher level than that of those who were committing the crimes. I still feel the same. When I published *Hoa Kiau di Indonesia* (*The Chinese in Indonesia*), I was immediately accused of being a traitor. As a result, they kept me in prison without a trial.

About love: Ever since I was young, everything I ever did was for Indonesia. Many people suggested that I should leave, but my roots are here. I can't live outside this country, even though if I were to live in the United States I would be paid between two and five thousand dollars for each appearance or speech [*laughs*].

But while you remain in Indonesia, you are enclosing yourself entirely within your own world...

I still think about Indonesia all the time, that's why I feel so much pain. I don't have any organization or my own media, so I keep everything inside. I can't write books anymore, so I can communicate what's inside me only when I get visitors like you.

Do you believe that the greatest service any writer can give to a nation is to reveal its flaws, even if it means exposing its darkest and most sinister secrets?

No. I discipline myself to see the world dialectically, so I don't portray only the dark side. I also try to show good aspects. If I only dealt with the darker elements, I'd probably become ill [*laughs*].

Do you sometimes wake up in the middle of the night, thinking about something that you forgot to say or write?

Even if I did, I no longer have the strength to correct it. I can't write a single line anymore. I've become a gong that only sounds when touched by other people. Don't forget, next year I'll turn eighty if I'm still alive. I know that there are people like Chomsky who are almost my age but still active, but they haven't lived such an abnormal life as me.

Which literary or philosophical figures influenced your writing? Whom do you really admire?

When I was young, I read the works of the Greek philosophers from Aristotle to Socrates. After that, I didn't read any other philosophers, because I got bored. I was influenced by

Maxim Gorki and John Steinbeck. I like Socialist Realism because it deals with social responsibilities.

As I mentioned before, in Buru I was saved by international monitors. That's why I have to reiterate my gratitude to the international community. Even my family was supported by some eminent people, including Günter Grass. At one time, Günter Grass urged the Indonesian government to release me, which led to his being deported from the country. That's him! I still keep his photograph on the wall. Later, in 1999, I met Günter Grass in Germany. When I returned to Indonesia after meeting him, I learned that he'd just received the Nobel Prize in Literature.

In what language have you read Maxim Gorki?

I read him in English and Dutch, but the English edition was published in Moscow.

Would you describe yourself as a Marxist?

No, I'm not a Marxist. I'm a "Pramist." I never follow any ideology or the teaching of others. I only follow my own beliefs. However, I do believe in social justice and equality.

Are you sure you'll write no more books?

I'm sure. I simply can't do it. I realized it eight years ago. Later, in the year 2000, I had a stroke while working in my field. I'd been working for a full hour when it began to rain very hard. I retired to the hut and slept there for some time, but when I opened my eyes, I saw the whole world in a purple color and realized that my strength was gone. When I tried to continue working, I found I couldn't even lift the shovel: all my strength had ebbed away.

I'm not able to write anything. I get letters from all over the world, but I can't respond to any of them.

How about articles for the newspapers and magazines?

I'm just filing everything. All I'm planning to publish, besides this book that we're working on now, is a collection of old letters. In the past, I wrote to many influential people, including President Clinton, but now I can't find the letter I sent to him. I was also collecting materials for an encyclopedia of the Indonesian archipelago that would offer in-depth information about its villages, cities, rivers, mountains, and oceans, but I can't finish that work, either.

If you still had enough strength to write, what would it be?

I don't have any desire to write anymore. I'm just waiting for my death to arrive. Many people have suggested that I speak and they would put my thoughts in writing, but I'm not used to teamwork. I feel I've already said all there was to say. The only thing that hurts me tremendously, the thing that I do want to discuss, is Indonesia's present terrible condition. It doesn't coincide with my childhood dreams, and that's why I agreed to write this book with you.

As I said, I can't write anymore, but I still have to sign many bills [*laughs*].

Chapter Five

Suharto's Regime and Indonesia Today

Can you explain the difference between the country that you and Sukarno envisaged when you were fighting for the independence of Indonesia and the country that you see now?

What we fought for and what is happening now are opposites—Suharto's intervention changed everything. The coalition between the military and the Golkar Party gave birth to the so-called Orde Baru—New Order—that was responsible for the deaths of approximately two million people. Only recently has the extent of the number of victims become apparent. The millions of murders committed by the military and Islamic groups were Suharto's route to power. In my opinion, the country of Indonesia is now in a process of decay and disintegration. It doesn't have a leader. From the time that Sukarno was ousted until the present, there has been no leadership. The young generation that deposed Suharto couldn't give birth to a leader, either. As a result, today's Indonesia has no direction.

*How would you summarize Suharto's dictatorship? How differ-
ent was it from Sukarno's vision?*

I see Suharto's Indonesia as limitless moral decadence. During the era of Sukarno, foreign capital had great difficulty in
entering Indonesia. After the coup, the doors were wide
open for foreign investors, and Suharto and others gained
enormous benefits from it. Suharto opened up Indonesia almost single-handedly, and what followed was plunder.

Right from the start, he worked closely with foreign
companies, including Freeport's investments in the gold
mines of Papua, from which he managed to get shares.
Freeport first announced that it would be exploiting copper
mines, but later a scientist from Bandung who worked for
them found out that, in reality, they were extracting gold.
He filed a report calling for a government investigation but
was fired shortly afterwards. Then someone broke into his
house and all his documents were stolen. Eventually, the scientist had to run for his life to the Middle East. Papua is
being ruined. The Freeport mining company alone has already destroyed three hills there.

However, I have no files, no direct proof. As foreign investment flowed into the country in an unstoppable stream,
Suharto got kickbacks and bribes from many different
sources. One of his children is now the biggest landowner in
Sumatra. What a bandit regime!

Suharto himself had no brains. His main driving force
was nothing more than a simple obsession with power that

in turn enabled him to accumulate tremendous wealth. Under his rule, Indonesia lost all its national pride and gained no achievements. None!

Anyway, he was no different than our current presidential candidates. What are their individual achievements? All they can do is talk. In my opinion, if Indonesians want to have progress, the very least they should have is some idea of a vision for Indonesia and the potential to aim at some personal achievements.

Suharto made sure that everything that Sukarno built was obliterated. He allowed the people's basest instincts to surface, especially their obsession with wealth and power. Everything was undermined by corruption. Even people's brains became corrupt.

Sukarno aimed at the opposite. His government is still the best we have experienced in Indonesia. Nevertheless, he managed to make many enemies among Western countries, because of his opposition to colonialism, capitalism, and imperialism. He always suspected that Western countries saw the rest of the world as their playing field, fit only for exploitation. That's why the West, led by the U.S., decided to support the coup against him.

But to answer your question, the main difference between Sukarno and Suharto was that Sukarno's era was marked by idealism, by his "nation and character building." He knew that this nation didn't yet have its own character or its own identity and that, unless it could develop them, Indonesia couldn't survive.

What was the impact of dictatorship and Suharto's economic policy on the lives of ordinary Indonesians? While traveling through this vast archipelago, we found that Indonesia—the fourth most populous nation on Earth—is collapsing. Misery is widespread. People have no voice and their lives have no alternatives. Public services are almost nonexistent. Corruption is rampant, and people can count on no protection from the judicial system or from the police. Education is often used only for political and religious indoctrination. In the past, Indonesia was easily competing with Malaysia and Thailand; now it has difficulties competing even with some of the poorest nations of Southeast Asia.

The Indonesian nation has become even poorer and more miserable. In the past, Indonesia was one of the biggest exporters of rice, but now we have to import it. Not only do we have to import it, but low-cost rice is also being smuggled in, and the result is that our farmers have to suffer. The same thing is happening with sugar. It's unbelievable. Domestic production is extremely low and underdeveloped. There is no agricultural policy in Indonesia—that's why everything is such a mess. We have to import toothpicks, ballot boxes, and even ink for the election marks. Can't they make it themselves? What a shame! We are a maritime country, but we have to import salt!

For many years, I've been asking myself how Indonesia became like this. I revisited history and finally arrived at the conclusion that the main problem has to be our low level of culture. Although it's obvious how mediocre it is, all Indonesian students were taught to glorify it. Another thing lacking is creative education, including education by families that could lead to some sort of production. All we've learned is how to consume—another legacy of Suharto's era. Indonesia doesn't produce.

We have to change our education at home and in schools: we have to learn how to create, how to build. If we learn how to produce, we'll also learn how to be truly independent. We'll be motivated to trade and to create things of value. However, if we don't have a decent system of education, how can we move forward? I don't know the answer, I really don't.

Oh, when we discuss the situation in Indonesia, I still feel as if I'm burning inside!

Indonesia should be a mighty nation because of its natural resources, but now it's nothing more than a nation of slaves. Indonesia's natural resources should have been used to make local people rich, but that never happened. Now local people are poor and enslaved. That's our culture, and it doesn't make me feel any better knowing that it has been like this since the sixteenth century.

It is no secret that the new Indonesian "elites" ignore the suffering of the great majority living in this nation. Would it be fair to compare Indonesian elites—those in managerial positions of today's multinational companies operating in Indonesia—to those who collaborated with the former colonial rule?

These are two different stories. During the colonial era, those who worked for the Dutch were respected by at least some Indonesians and Europeans. Now it's different. Those who work for foreign companies are just servants and everybody knows it. In the past, those who worked with the Dutch administration had some status, at least, but that's not true of today's servants. When I was still young, our dream was to go to school, learn the Dutch language, and then get a job as a civil servant.

It would be incorrect to put all the blame for post-1965 developments on Suharto. It would make everything much easier, but wouldn't it be escapism? No doubt that Suharto was the main player, but thousands, probably millions, were benefiting from the regime. Many were helping to shape it. Who were really the main players in post-1965 Indonesia?

Suharto was the mastermind, of course. He is responsible for the downfall of our nation. Sukarno was a visionary, but all his concepts were crushed by Suharto and his gang. Later, New Order gave birth to a new version of New Order, but even then, administrative power rested in Suharto's hands. That's why nobody has dared to bring him to trial up to now. Suharto built his system on Javanese fascist principles.

It seems that corruption touches every aspect of Indonesian life. Corruption is part of the government; of the military, police, and judiciary; of big business and the mass media; of political parties and religious movements. It seems that an ordinary Indonesian citizen can hardly take a single step without having to bribe someone. How did this happen? What are the roots of this kleptocracy?

Those who are corrupt and those who are corrupting have no culture of production. They are spineless. Corruption became a social epidemic. People are obsessed with extracting money from each other. It's shameful. People are begging, and when it doesn't work, they threaten.

Corruption cases, even the most obvious ones, are hardly ever brought before a court. Look at the case of Akbar Tanjung,* for example. It was never investigated, and no one discovered what happened to the forty billion rupiah that he pocketed. The money just disappeared. Isn't Indonesia great for people like him? He was even going to run for president!

Everybody is talking about the corrupt officials in Suharto's and post-Suharto Indonesia. Who are they? What's their background?

It starts with the leadership, the elites, and with those in high positions in the bureaucracy. In Indonesia, bureaucrats who don't hold high positions are regarded as dirt. It starts with the way that all these people think. It's significant that their brains are rotten—corruption itself is then just a mechanical act, a habit. These people have no idea how to produce. Throughout their lives, all they've ever done is to do what they were told. They want to become wealthy without having to work. In Indonesia, almost everyone who doesn't produce is corrupt.

In Sukarno's era, corruption already existed, albeit on a relatively small scale, but after 1965 it became part of daily life in Indonesia. Why?

* See Glossary

Yes, that's correct. Corruption under Sukarno was on a much smaller scale. Later, under Suharto's dictatorship, Indonesia lost its purpose as a nation, and the national struggle disappeared. You also have to remember that in his era, Suharto himself was the most corrupt person in Indonesia, he and his children. Yet there was never any lawsuit against him or his family, a clear example of Javanism. After he lost power, millions of people decided to follow his example. Their primitive logic told them: if the head of the state could do it and get away with it, why shouldn't we?

When Sukarno was still in power, almost all of us were involved in nation and character building. For me, these ideas still represent the foundations on which my understanding of the world is built. I tried to incorporate this idea of nation and character building into all my books.

So large-scale corruption started at the top, with Suharto himself?

Of course! Where else could his enormous wealth have come from? Originally, he was just a sergeant in the KNIL [Royal Dutch Indies Army].* When Sukarno put Suharto in charge of an antismuggling unit, Suharto himself became involved in smuggling goods from Indonesia to Singapore. This fact is documented in a letter from Subandrio* to Sukarno.

In earlier days, Sukarno had some sympathy for Suharto because he was involved in the fight for Yogyakarta* in the days of the liberation struggle. Suharto used that sympathy only for his personal gain.

* See Glossary

Why did Suharto's dictatorship eliminate Indonesian intellectuals? It seems that almost one-half of Indonesian teachers lost their lives in the 1965 purges. Film studios and publishing houses were closed down; artists were thrown into prisons and silenced.

As I said before, Suharto is a fascist. His main weapon was fear. Even killing two million people after the coup was, in reality, some sort of warning, an act intended to make the nation petrified. His goal was to silence any voice of dissent, to make everyone kneel in front of him. Yes—the cost was two million human lives, not to mention those who were thrown into prisons and the terrible fate that awaited their families. It was all about fear …

Elections seem to be a farce. The majority of people we encounter—from Java to Flores—have no idea whom to vote for, as the candidates don't even bother to explain their political program. It is doubtful they have any, apart from their personal and party interests. How do you see the present-day political system in Indonesia?

To start with, I don't believe in an electoral process anymore. And here, none of the Indonesian presidential candidates really addresses important issues: none of them has a vision for this country.

Are all the great ideas on which Indonesia was supposed to be built really gone?

Yes, and now, when all the values have disappeared, the Indonesian archipelago, from Aceh to Papua, is a total mess.

By the way, Papua used to be called Irian, but when Gus Dur [former president Abdurahman Wahid] came to power, he changed its name to Papua. Irian was a good name: it's an abbreviation of Ini Republik Indonesia Anti Nederland [This is the Republic of Indonesia against the Netherlands].

How do you view the invasion and occupation of East Timor by Indonesian troops during Suharto's rule? It is disturbing to realize that until now, the Indonesian public had no knowledge of the atrocities—they believed that it was a regular war where "they were killing us and we were killing them."

East Timor was occupied because Suharto decided to invade.

Sukarno, on the other hand, always refused any suggestion to take it over, because he always regarded Indonesia as a group of islands that were formerly a Dutch colony, while East Timor was colonized by the Portuguese. For Sukarno, this issue was a matter of principle, but Suharto saw East Timor as a weak, defenseless country, easy to grab.

During my time in the Buru concentration camp, we were often visited by army generals. They kept lecturing us. One of them was bragging repeatedly about the capability of Indonesia to take over East Timor in two hours. I laughed to his face. It was obvious he didn't realize that even years wouldn't settle the issue or break resistance to the occupation. They didn't anticipate that they would have to face determined guerrillas and simple people there. In the end, the occupation and war lasted for dozens of years, not two hours, and our generals lost!

I fully agree that East Timor should be free and independent from Indonesia. Since the very beginning, I always maintained this view. They have a different administrative structure and cultural experience from us.

Adam Malik, the foreign minister of Indonesia, said in 1977: "50,000 people or perhaps 80,000 people might have been killed during the war in East Timor…. It was a war…. [W]hat is the big fuss?" This reflects the attitude of the government toward the slaughter in its colony. Do you see what happened as a part of the culture of terror under Suharto's dictatorship?

Yes. It was Suharto who was responsible for the killing. We Indonesians simply refuse to learn from our own history. One brutality followed another, and even now, this is happening in Aceh. I have to repeat again and again that I see Indonesia as a body in the process of decay.

How could the military manage to kill over 30 percent of the population of East Timor?

They had the experience, didn't they? They had plenty of experience fighting defenseless people in their own country in Indonesia after 1965. They had no moral scruples. The objective of forming a military is to fight foreign enemies. Domestic problems should be resolved by a police force, but in Indonesia they fight their own people. If a foreign enemy decided to attack our country, they would probably be able to conquer it in a few days because our military would be useless.

After fighting unarmed people in Indonesia, they continued killing civilians in tiny East Timor. This is the main problem: our military has different principles from you and me.

How is it possible that the Indonesian public still knows nothing, or next to nothing, about what happened in East Timor?

It was all a matter of politics. The mass media were, and still are, controlled by those in power. If they were not in line with the rulers of the country, they would be banned and closed down. It's all very simple.

But there is one place in Indonesia for which you feel admiration …

As far as I'm concerned, not all of Indonesia is rotting: Aceh is an exception! When Indonesia had already been colonized by the Dutch for two hundred years, the Acehnese were still independent and fighting the invaders. They are really individualists. To conquer Aceh, the Dutch sent assassins from Java, and the Indonesian state continues to do the same now. That's why I've always said that the Indonesian people have to learn from the Acehnese, from their spirit of individualism. Yes, the Acehnese are brave: they are taught to be like that by their families.

Today, even women are fighting in Aceh. During the Dutch occupation, a single Acehnese fighter would sneak into a compound and blow it up. That could have never happened in Java. In my opinion, the Indonesian government is not capable of resolving the mess it created in Aceh, just as it was unable to solve problems in East Timor. That's why I'm calling for an international tribunal to arbitrate the conflict in Aceh and decide who is responsible for the war crimes there. However, so far my calls have not been met by any response.

Chapter Six

American Involvement

Indonesia managed to kill millions of its own people after the coup of 1965, in Aceh, Papua, Ambon, and elsewhere. On the other hand, the United States doesn't usually kill its own people en masse but helps to destroy nations and kill millions in foreign lands by following its economic and geopolitical interests. Which do you consider more evil?

Both, of course [*laughs*]! By the way, don't forget that the Americans massacred their own indigenous population and then, after they finished, probably thought that the rest of the world was inhabited by "Red Indians" too, so they just continued with the same policy.

Seriously, had Sukarno not been deposed by the U.S., the present world would be a very different place. It's such a shambles now. Although I was personally helped by American people when I was in prison and my books were banned in Indonesia, I consider U.S. foreign policy to be a total disaster! Iraq, for example! What are they doing there—occupying it? Even here in Indonesia, the Americans used to bomb the Molucca Islands during the Sukarno era.

What role did the U.S. and the West play in Suharto's dictatorship? The Americans got everything they wanted: great deals for their multinational companies, often signed—after substantial bribes—by Suharto himself; an obedient workforce; a society which never dared to openly revolt. Papua and Aceh—areas with tremendous natural wealth—had been brutally oppressed. Billions of dollars in forcefully dispersed foreign loans—which disappeared in corruption—assured that Indonesia lost its economic independence. Indonesia became so anticommunist that even words like "atheism" and "class" (referring to the social classes) were banned.

The role was played by capital—by money! Western countries wanted to convert the world, including Indonesia, into their playground. In reality, in Indonesia that was very difficult to achieve because of the culture of corruption here. Elites here couldn't be trusted, so their plans failed.

What was their strategy for securing the cooperation of the Indonesian military?

They trained Indonesian military personnel in the United States. They supplied them with weapons and, of course, many high-ranking military officers were indoctrinated in an American way of thinking. Indoctrination itself has had an enormous impact on this society, especially the anticommunist sentiments implanted by the United States.

This sort of indoctrination is conducted by the United States all over the world. There is nothing democratic about it, despite the fact that the U.S. tries to present itself as a democratic society.

Back in Indonesia, after being indoctrinated, our military did the killing. The U.S. was betting on the right horse: the military is the only organization that can perform extermination on such a scale.

It all sounds like an old song, doesn't it? The U.S. attacks many countries all over the world, so it's not a big deal for them to destroy one or two.

To what extent can the U.S. be blamed for the 1965–1966 killings in Indonesia?

The extent of the U.S.'s culpability isn't clear to me. One thing that's obvious is that the U.S. never condemned the massacres. Never! In fact, the Western media welcomed those events enthusiastically. I think that there was cooperation between the U.S. and the Indonesian military during the killing, but I have no concrete proof.

Nowadays, documents disclosing this cooperation are appearing, especially in Holland. However, based on what you said, the American public doesn't know much about what happened here in Indonesia and about the involvement of its own country. That's because Americans never pay much attention to foreign affairs, maybe because they consider themselves superior to people from other nations. Look at what's happening in Iraq—and they may invade other countries in the near future, too!

I'm sure that the issue of U.S. involvement in the 1965 coup in Indonesia was covered by at least some of the progressive and specialized publications in America. Even my own writing is well known in the United States. Ironically, some publishing houses in Asia still refuse to publish my work. However, that's never happened in America: they've always published my books there. I have no idea if the American public accepts my point of view, but last month my book *Tales from Blora* appeared on the bookshelves there, and it's selling well.

Some documents show, and several scholars believe, that the U.S. and the Indonesian military were planning the 1965 coup together.

The mightiest weapon of the United States has always been its dollar: don't forget that, and don't forget that Eisenhower, then the U.S. president, ordered the deposing of Sukarno. Eisenhower himself gave the speech underlining this issue. The CIA used Suharto. The United States had enormous influence over the Indonesian military and, later, over Golkar. Even when we were political prisoners, we knew that the United States had been behind everything that happened.

What interests were involved? Why was the U.S. so eager to help Suharto?

It all happened because they wanted to depose Sukarno. During the Cold War, Sukarno refused to side with the West, while maintaining excellent relations with the People's

Republic of China. Since China was a Communist country, Sukarno was considered an enemy by the West and thus had to be deposed. As I just said, even President Eisenhower made no secrets about it. Can you imagine it? A president of one country openly saying that the president of another sovereign country should be deposed!

After the decision had been made, the rest was just a job for the CIA. For the West, the main issue in 1965 was how to get rid of Sukarno.

After that happened, all Sukarno's supporters were thrown into prison or murdered. Western involvement in Indonesia in 1965 was directly linked to the Cold War. Those who suffered the most were Communists. I had also been accused of being a Communist, although that's rubbish! A Sukarno supporter, yes, but not a Communist. I'm a Pramist!

Would right-wing forces and the military in Indonesia have been able to carry out the coup without the U.S. determination to depose Sukarno?

It would be almost unthinkable. Sukarno was loved by his people.

Before 1965, was there any visible influence or mingling of the United States in Indonesian affairs?

Of course. The United States bombed Indonesian territory from their bases in the Philippines—and they never apologized for attacking us directly!

Which part of Indonesian territory was bombed?

Our northern islands near the Philippine archipelago.

What was the reaction of the Indonesian government and military? Did they try to defend their territory?

During one bombing mission, the Indonesian forces managed to shoot down an airplane and capture the pilot, Allan Poe. However, as many Indonesian military officers were trained in the United States, what else could you expect? Nothing happened.

I'm an admirer of Ho Chi Minh. He led a peasant rebellion that grew to a revolution and drove both France and the U.S. from his country. The U.S. was furious when the Vietnamese decided to go their own way and then overcame their invasion! Later, they tried to prevent Indonesia from becoming another Vietnam—that's what it was all about.

Was it an act of intimidation, or did they bomb some particular targets for specific reasons?

The bombing was performed to give moral support to the people of the Moluccas, who were trying to secede from Indonesia. Most of the people from Sulawesi and the Moluccas are of Christian faith, and there seemed to be a link between them and the United States. In addition, the United States has an historic animosity toward Islam—you can see it even now.

The United States should have helped us to build democracy, instead of teaching us terrible lessons that we never asked for. How can one help with building democracy in another country? First, one has to act democratically oneself; one has to set an example.

Chapter Seven

Reconciliation?

Between one and three million people died in massacres and purges in Indonesia after 1965. The ruling elites are now proposing to set up some sort of reconciliation process. But they want to do it on their own conditions, as they never really lost power. Is it possible to achieve reconciliation when the past is not yet acknowledged, the system which sent millions to prison and to death is still in place, and while victims haven't been offered any compensation?

Reconciliation in Indonesia is not possible. Even to think about it is a joke. People have been victimized. What our military and civil elites would like to do is to disregard the entire legal process. If they want reconciliation, how is it that nothing that was confiscated from me and from others has ever been returned? Not even my old house!

What kind of reconciliation are they proposing? In my case, eight manuscripts were destroyed—they can never be replaced. The main problem is that nobody is claiming responsibility for these acts, and that includes Suharto himself. I refuse to pay taxes in Indonesia unless they compensate me for everything they have taken from me. Once they summoned me to the tax office and I said to them, "First give me back all that you took away from me!"

So, even before proposing reconciliation, they should at least recognize the past, admit their crimes, conduct real trials with those who were responsible for killing and other atrocities, and apologize to the victims.

Exactly! The most important is to have trials. If this country has no respect for the law, then it's better to forget the whole thing—forget reconciliation! Even courts here can't be trusted. In this country, everything is damaged.

You can see what they did to my life. My manuscripts were confiscated or destroyed, and they meant everything to me. All my books were banned, and I was arrested. I've been thrown into prisons and camps and finally locked in house arrest. All that went on for thirty-four years, and all that without a trial! How can they propose reconciliation? It's sick!

Those who did the killing are now suggesting reconciliation with the victims. These suggestions are now even coming from some people belonging to Nahdlatul Ulama [NU, an organization of Muslim scholars].*

Indonesians are now learning a new expression: human rights. That's very new here, unbelievably. The subject is so new that it's discussed only among intellectuals. Maybe they

* See Glossary

should learn much more about it before we start any serious discussion about reconciliation.

"Gus Dur"—the former president of Indonesia, Abdurahman Wahid—told us recently that he has tremendous respect for you and is planning to create a foundation in your name. This foundation is supposed to help the victims of 1965 and their families. Do you have some hope that it can make a difference?

Because he used to be a chairperson of NU, Gus Dur feels responsible for the past. He feels guilty, even though he is not personally responsible for the killings. That's good, but the problem is that Gus Dur is again getting close to the military because he is looking for political support before the elections. At the least, he is looking for their protection. All our politicians are opportunists.

Have you ever thought about suing the military or the government? After all, you can have a tremendous case against them: unlawful and long imprisonment, destruction of your manuscripts, confiscation of your home …

I actually tried: I tried to get back the house that the military confiscated from me. It was pointless. My case was closely watched by over three hundred victims who were ready to fight for their confiscated property if I succeeded—they were from Jakarta alone. But I failed! All Sukarno supporters experienced a similar fate. Anyone who dares to face the military is silenced. That time I decided to act as an *enfant terrible*—I wanted them to put me on trial, but even that plan failed.

When we discussed the things that you lost, didn't you say they also burned your library?

They did. They burned my library and all my documents. At that time, there were no photocopiers, and all manuscripts and documents were typed. Everything disappeared.

Chapter Eight

Revolution:
The Future of Indonesia

Can you think of any leader whom you could vote for in the forthcoming presidential elections?

None of the presidential candidates has any concept for Indonesia, no vision. What can we expect from them? They are like clowns. For example, our Indonesian forests are being plundered, but no candidate is addressing this issue. The wealth at the bottom of our oceans is being stolen too. We even used to export sand, until several of our islands disappeared. Officially supported imports, as well as smuggling, robbed millions of Indonesians of their jobs. Everything is out of control, and the further from the main islands you go, the worse it becomes. However, none of the candidates addresses these or other important issues.

What do you think will happen to Indonesia if General Wiranto—a war criminal—becomes the president of the country?

Let me say this before answering your question. In order to become president of Indonesia, one should have some vision for the country. Second, one should have some individual achievements. If they don't have either of those qualities, how can they lead the country?

Now, if the president comes from the military, Indonesia will be in a much worse condition, considering how much power the army already has. If a soldier wins the election, I will probably be thrown back into prison. I have known the Indonesian army since the revolution. For a time I was in their ranks as a second lieutenant, so I know how they operate.

Does it really matter who becomes the president of Indonesia? It seems that it is elites and the military who are still controlling the nation. Do you care if it is Megawati or Susilo Bambang Yudhoyono sitting in Istana Negara?

No matter which of these people you mentioned is in power, the pitiful conditions in Indonesia will remain.

We agree. But then what can change the situation?

Only the young generation can answer this question, not me. Since 1915, Indonesian history had been written by the young generations. I can't act anymore. All I can do now is speak. There has to be a young-generation movement. But instead of making changes, I've noticed that many young people prefer to go straight to the bank and ask for a loan to buy a motorcycle so they can become *ojek** drivers.

* See Glossary

They don't care about producing or changing things; all they want to do is to drive around the block and collect some money. It's the polar opposite of China, where people know how to produce things and how to sell them. If I were in power, I would immediately impose quotas on imports and cut all imports by 50 percent, so there would be new jobs for Indonesians, and they would finally be forced to produce.

I gather you don't particularly support Indonesian-style capitalism?

Capitalism is the same everywhere. Its only purpose is to make as high a profit as it is allowed to. I believe in each country's right to self-determination, but, in reality, such rights are not being honored. Everything is determined by big business, even the fate of nations.

Can the present situation change without a revolution?

It can't. There has to be a revolution!

After 1965, there was destruction and only destruction, and it continues until now. The system can't be fixed, only dismantled. Government officials become thieves the very moment they get their positions. The law increasingly resembles a commodity-trading bazaar.

Covering the downfall of Suharto in 1998, I moved to Trisakti University, the headquarters of the student uprising. One thing that surprised me was that the student leaders were rebelling

only against Suharto's government and what they called "crony-
ism," not against the backward culture, oppressive family struc-
ture, religious interference in the daily life of Indonesian citi-
zens; not even against the political and economic system as such.
It was nothing like 1968 in Paris or Mexico City, where stu-
dents began a massive rebellion against the entire culture, soci-
ety, and political system.

That's exactly what was called *reformasi,* an attempt to reform Suharto's New Order. To reform New Order would
just have created an upgraded version of the old New Order.
It would have had nothing to do with a real revolution.

I believe our young generation has no idea about real
revolution. The movements after 1998 were attempting to
reform New Order, the very same system that destroyed
Sukarno, killed millions of people, and interrupted the natural development of Indonesia.

Pram, are you an internationalist? Do you think that Indonesia
can ever have a successful revolution without any outside help?

Indonesia succeeded in revolutions in the past, without any
outside help. However, in today's world, nobody can escape
foreign interventions, and to go it alone would be much
more difficult. Even so, I'm convinced that a country can
carry out a revolution without outside help. It depends on
the country's capabilities and determination.

In our case, for example, our neighboring countries, including Malaysia, give us more problems than help. They
add to the destruction of our forests through illegal logging,

instead of supporting our revolutions. When there was a rebellion by PRRI/PERMESTA,* our neighboring countries provided them with arms. That's why I don't have much trust in our neighbors.

Do you have faith in any international organization or movement? Do you support the efforts of the World Social Forum?

This organization is still only in the talking stage, not an acting one. They have very good intentions, but what concrete actions have they taken? From my point of view, even demonstrations and protests are not more than talk.

But what kind of concrete action can be taken in Indonesia?

A revolution that would help to get rid of those who are in the way of natural Indonesian development. That's why I told you that those who would like to become presidents of this country should first have a vision for this country. The reason why Indonesia is in such a mess is that all our candidates are acting in their own interests. That's why. We have no real leaders, no one that can show the way.

Suharto's dictatorship was closely connected to the global dictatorship. It is sometimes called "The New World Order" or "globalization." In this system, Indonesia had been both victim and victimizer. Victim, because its system had been destroyed—partially with help from outside—during and after 1965. Victimizer, because of Javanese colonialism itself and the terrible treatment of

* See Glossary

*the territories it is occupying, including East Timor, Papua, and
Aceh. Can this system—this global system—be fought?*

Today, everything here is controlled by a desire to make
profit. It's part of the global system, and that system is
wrong. To fight against it, we have to organize some sort of
global struggle. A global system has to be fought by global
resistance, and if we can't fight it in the open, at least for now
we can try to tame it and reshape it for the benefit of the
great majority of the people living on this planet.

*But then, referring to the question above, do you think that In-
donesia can fight this enormous system alone?*

Indonesia can have its own revolution, but in order to fight a
global economic and political dictatorship, it needs to have
allies. First, how can we unite as a nation fighting global
power if our own government and elites can't be trusted?
They take sides only with those who grease their palms.
That's the reality of Indonesia. That's why we first need to
have our own revolution: only then can we look for allies for
a global struggle.

*How do you see the Indonesian government and elites? Are they
just a bunch of servants of foreign interests?*

Yes, they are servants. Now you can understand why I'm
burning inside! Geographically, Indonesia is still united, but
it is divided socially. Indonesia is in extremely bad shape: it's
sick! We are sick, terminally ill, and the only medicine is rev-

olution—the revolution that Sukarno was never allowed to complete.

I'm not trying to inflame the situation, but the conditions under which Indonesia exists are calling for the revolution. It's all in the hands of the younger generation. The older generation with its ideas is just a burden, and that probably includes me as well [*laughs*].

Is there a social, economic, or political structure in the world that you would consider suitable, some sort of model that Indonesia could follow?

It's difficult to find one, even in Europe. Europeans failed so many times. Look at Germany and Hitler. There, they managed to kill millions of people. In turn, massacres in Europe led to the birth of the state of Israel, a new country created by European Jews. But look what Israel is doing now to Palestinians!

But socially, I think that the present European system could be used as an example for Indonesia.

Maybe one day we can create our own concept, but this country still has no sound concepts apart from obedience to power. All other concepts were imported from Europe or elsewhere: nothing is indigenous. I'm not proud of my ancestors. Hell, it's all messed up! That's why I keep talking and talking to young people, urging them to form their own culture and get rid of our old ancestral culture.

After talking for several days, it seems that you really see no other solution than a revolution.

Exactly—a revolution! It's the only medicine. I have to repeat again and again that Indonesia is rotting. There's corruption and bureaucracy, the two main symptoms of the
sickness. In terms of the economy, there is almost no production but an enormous thirst for consumption. Families
don't educate their children and don't teach them how to
produce. It is now so bad that only a revolution can save the
nation. I think that Indonesia has reached a point beyond
salvation unless there is radical change. It has to be led by
our youth: they should just stop talking about it and do it!
The only answer is revolution—there is no other option.

But what kind of revolution?

Total revolution!

*Should Indonesia start all over again—from the beginning—as
it did in 1945?*

Yes, it has to start all over again. Now everything is too damaged, so no reforms can be effective. What can we do if the
entire administrative power is in the hands of Golkar, if real
power is in the hands of the military and elites who are stealing all that is left of Indonesia and selling it abroad? What
can be done? The answer is revolution. Total revolution!

Chapter Nine

Before Parting

Where does Indonesia fit into the world today?

What can I say about the world? We hardly know anything about the world here, and the world knows nothing about Indonesia. In Southeast Asia, Indonesia's reputation is one of a sick person, and that stigma doesn't go away. For my part, I've done everything I could for Indonesia, but look what it did to me in return. My books have been translated into thirty-six languages, but I have never been respected in Indonesia itself. I'm respected abroad but not here. When I was in the middle of the struggle against this system, ironically it was America that honored me with awards. Then I received support and recognition from other countries, but never from my own nation.

Based on what you just declared, did you make your decision to remain silent because you felt that you had nothing to add to what you'd already said and written, or because you were hurt by your country and its culture?

It's much simpler. I really can't write anymore. I know my limits and I've reached them, so I have to stop here. I want to stop dreaming. That's the tragedy of an old age and I'm not complaining, because when I was young, I never even imagined that I could reach this age. My experience in Buru hardened me, but now I'm tired.

I live within myself. I can't do anything about it. I can talk freely only when my friends come to visit me. When I think about Indonesia, I feel a burning inside me, and it never goes away.

So you live in internal exile?

Yes, in internal exile, in my own world. Outside my world, there is only corruption. Sukarno, our leader, is no more. Since I was a young man, I've given everything I had to Indonesia, and now I believe that I've already given enough. Nothing good came back in return. The country for which I fought is now decaying, so how could I not feel wrath? It became the exact opposite of the dreams of my youth. These days, so many memories come back to me. Most of the people I knew are gone. Two million human beings were murdered and rivers were clogged with dead bodies. How can people kill others just like that? I can't talk about it anymore. It's too emotional.

Let's stop here …

Glossary

George Aditjondro A leading Indonesian critic of Indonesia's occupation of East Timor and suppression of democracy, Dr. George Aditjondro lives in exile in Australia. He now lectures in sociology at Newcastle University.

Golkar (abbr.) Golongan Karya, the main political vehicle of Suharto's dictatorship until 1999. In the 2004 legislative elections, the Golkar Party gained 21.6 percent of the popular vote and again became the biggest party in the Indonesian parliament. Its present leader is Akbar Tanjung: he is currently accused of corruption.

KNIL Koninklijk Nederlands-Indisch Leger, or the Royal Dutch Indies Army.

Manikebu A "Cultural Manifesto" advocating cultural freedom without limits and universal humanism.

Multatuli Pseudonym of the nineteenth-century Dutch writer Eduard Douwes Dekker.

Nahdlatul Ulama, NU (Revival of Ulama), a Muslim Scholars' Organization. Founded on January 31, 1926, with a goal to maintain and develop Ahlussunnah-wal-Jamaah Islamic teachings and follow one of the four *madzhab* [schools of thought] in Islam under the Pancasila and the 1945 constitution. By the end of 1965, a huge wave of popular violence against the PKI was under way. In west and central Java, the army began rounding up Communists, but in many villages, people took the law into their own hands. In some areas, such as East Java and Aceh, Islamic groups (such as the Nahdlatul Ulama youth group Ansor) fought to wipe out Communists.

Ojek A motorcycle or bicycle used as public transport.

Orde Baru (New Order) The title adopted by Suharto's regime.

Pancasila "Five Principles" that were the official ideology of post-independence Indonesia under Sukarno: belief in God, nationalism, humanitarianism, social justice, and democracy.

PETA Pembela Tanah Air. An Indonesian youth defense force recruited by the Japanese during the occupation.

PRRI/PERMESTA Revolutionary Government of the Republic of Indonesia/Universal Struggle Charter. The charter was adopted by sections of the Indonesian army who staged an unsuccessful revolt against the Sukarno government in 1958.

Dr. Subandrio Indonesian foreign minister under Sukarno.

Sudomo Admiral Sudomo was the coordinating minister for political affairs and security during the Suharto regime.

Sumpah Pemuda The "Oath of the Youth." On October 28, 1928, an Indonesian movement of youths from various ethnic groups and religions vowed to create a single motherland on Indonesian soil: one nation, Indonesia, and one language, Indonesian.

Sutan Syahrir Leader of the Socialist Party of Indonesia (PSI) during the Sukarno years.

Akbar Tanjung Tanjung, who leads the notoriously corrupt Golkar Party, was convicted of corruption in September 2002 and sentenced to three years in jail. He strongly denied any wrongdoing and remained free pending his lengthy appeals process.

The Central Jakarta District Court had found him guilty of misappropriating Rp40 billion (about $4.7 million) in state funds from the National Logistics Agency (Bulog). The money was supposed to have been used to buy food for the needy. Tanjung had allegedly received Rp40 billion in 10

Bulog checks over March–April 1999 when he was state sec-
retary/cabinet secretary under then president B. J. Habibie.

Source: www.laksamana.net

Tomy Winata and *Tempo* magazine Tomy Winata is an
ethnic Chinese banking and real estate mogul and one of Indonesia's most successful, powerful, and well-connected businessmen. Critics argue that he is also one of the nation's
most crooked tycoons, given his ties to the underworld and
the military, his use of hired thugs, and his penchant for giving "donations" to officials. In March 2003, *Tempo* magazine
published an article headlined "Ada Tomy di Tenabang?" (Is
Tomy in Tanah Abang?) that referred to Winata as a "scav-
enger extraordinaire." The article implied that Winata stood
to benefit from a February 2003 fire that had destroyed
about fifty-five hundred kiosks at the huge Tanah Abang textile market in central Jakarta. Winata filed a libel lawsuit
against *Tempo*.

The article, written by Ahmad Taufik, quoted an un-
named architectural contractor as saying that in December
2002, Winata had made a proposal to the Jakarta administration for a Rp53 billion ($5.9 million) project to renovate
the sprawling Tanah Abang complex, the largest textile market in Southeast Asia. Taufik devoted several paragraphs to
Winata's denial of any involvement in the plan to renovate
the market, but the tycoon still felt that *Tempo* had unfairly
damaged his "good name."

The Central Jakarta District Court ordered the PT
Tempo Intimedia Tbk (the *Tempo* publishing group) to pay

Rp500 million ($58,580) to Winata for defaming him in a magazine article and rejected a counter-suit filed by *Tempo* against Winata.

The ruling was the second time that Winata had won a lawsuit against PT Tempo Intimedia Tbk during 2002. On January 20, 2004, the East Jakarta District Court handed down a record libel judgment against *Koran Tempo,* another paper owned by the publishing group. The daily was ordered to pay $1 million in damages to Winata for an article suggesting that he was planning to open an illegal casino (gambling is prohibited in Indonesia but is widely tolerated by crooked officials). The court found that the daily had violated the Press Law and the journalistic code of ethics, and said that the article had been based only on rumor and hearsay. *Tempo* has filed an appeal against the verdict.

Source: www.laksamana.net

The Fight for Yogyakarta In a personal communication with the authors, Asvi Warman Adam writes: "Sukarno initially respected Suharto because of his commendable service when he led an attack on the Dutch in Yogyakarta. The attack lasted only several hours, but it was enough to send a message to the outside world that the Republic of Indonesia still existed even though Sukarno and Hatta had been captured by the Dutch. As a result, the United Nations (UN) agreed to discuss 'Indonesian issues' again. In the New Order era, this attack was glorified and two monuments were erected in Yogyakarta to remember it, but it was a controversial issue as the role of Sri Sultan Hamengku Buwono IX was left out by Suharto's supporters. In fact, this attack was created and planned by Sri Sultan Hamengku Buwono IX—at that time state minister for defense. Suharto was just the field officer. Sri Sultan Hamengku Buwono IX heard from foreign radio that the UN was going to convene. In anticipation, Sri Sultan thought that it was really important to tell the world that Indonesia still existed even though the Dutch had arrested the president and vice president. He planned an attack in Yogyakarta, which was occupied by the Dutch, and asked Suharto to come to his palace, kraton Yogyakarta. Before doing this, Sri Sultan had informed General Sudirman—at that time chief of the army—and he agreed with the plan.

Chronology

	role officer every month.
1988	Wins the PEN Freedom-to-Write Award.
1992	Stops reporting to military authorities.
1995	Receives the prestigious Ramon Magsaysay Award.
2004	Receives the Norwegian Authors' Union Award.

Selected Works

	1990), Buru Quartet, vol. 3
1988	*Rumah Kaca* (*House of Glass*, trans. Max Lane, 1992), Buru Quartet, vol. 4
1995	*Nyanyi Sunyi Seorang Bisu I*
1997	*Nyanyi Sunyi Seorang Bisu II*
2000	*The Mute's Soliloquy: A Memoir* (trans. Willem Samuels)
2002	*The Girl from the Coast* (trans. Willem Samuels)

Authors

Andre Vltchek is a Czech-American novelist, investigative journalist, and filmmaker. He is a co-founder of Mainstay Press (www.mainstaypress.org), a publishing house specializing in progressive political fiction, and is a senior fellow at the Oakland Institute (www.oaklandinstitute.org). Ande is the author of several novels including, most recently, *Point of No Return*, as well as a book of political essays, *Western Terror: From Potosi to Baghdad*. He produced and directed a 90-minute documentary, *Terlena—Breaking of a Nation,* about the brutality of Suharto's dictatorship. He has covered numerous conflicts for independent and mainstream media, including those in Peru, Mexico, Sri Lanka, India, Indonesia, East Timor, Fiji, and Thailand. He presently lives and works in Southeast Asia and the South Pacific.

Rossie Indira is an architect, business analyst, and writer. She writes for the *Jakarta Post* and *Gatra* in Indonesia. She is also co-author of *Saya Terbakar Amarah Sendirian: Pramoedya Ananta Toer dalam perbincangan dengan Andre Vltchek & Rossie Indira* (KPG, Indonesia). She is the production manager, translator, and advisor of a 90-minute documentary *Terlena—Breaking of a Nation* about the brutality of Suharto's dictatorship.

Contributors

Chris GoGwilt is professor of English and comparative literature at Fordham University in New York. He has written extensively on Pramoedya's work and is the author of *The Fiction of Geopolitics: Afterimages of Culture, from Wilkie Collins to Alfred Hitchcock* (Stanford University Press).

Nagesh Rao is assistant professor of English at The College of New Jersey, where he teaches postcolonial literature. His research on postcolonial literature and theory has appeared in several journals, including *Race and Class*, *South Asian Review,* and *Postcolonial Text.*